FOR
FREEDOM
DESTINED

BY THE SAME AUTHOR

Man: The Bridge Between Two Worlds
The Psychology of Leadership
National Psychology in International Relations

FOR FREEDOM DESTINED

Mysteries of Man's Evolution in Wagner's Ring Operas and Parsifal

FRANZ E. WINKLER

Introduction and Narrative Reductions of the Operas by M.G.H. Gilliam

Illustrations by Elizabeth de Jong

MYRIN INSTITUTE BOOKS
New York

Contents

About the Author   vii

Wagner's Artistic Ideal:
An Introductory Comment   ix

FOR FREEDOM DESTINED

 I. The Mythology in Wagner's *Rhinegold* 1

 II. The Mythology in Wagner's *Valkyrie* 19

 III. The Mythology in Wagner's *Seigfried* 35

 IV. The Mythology in Wagner's
   Twilight of the Gods 55

 V. The Mythology in Wagner's *Parsifal* 77

Appendix:
NARRATIVE REDUCTIONS OF THE OPERAS 107

 The Rhinegold 109

 The Valkyrie 118

 Siegfried 129

 The Twilight of the Gods 145

 Parsifal 160

 Notes 176

About the Author

FRANZ E. WINKLER, M.D.
April 12, 1907-January 1, 1972

Shortly before his death, Franz E. Winkler commented that perhaps more than any of his other writings and lectures, those dealing with the mythology of Wagner's Ring operas and *Parsifal* could kindle, particularly among the younger generation, an understanding of the meaning of life. Dr. Winkler gave this series of lectures during the years 1964-1967, later revising them for use as articles published in the *Proceedings* of the Myrin Institute for Adult Education. He intended to have them reprinted under one cover but did not live to see this project realized.

Winkler's lifelong interest in human psychology, coupled with his ability to treat not only physical ailments but also the various problems of life confronting his patients, distinguished him in his medical practice. As a student in Austria, he specialized in internal medicine under the Viennese physicians Wenckebach and Eppinger and in psychiatry under Wagner von Jauregg, Freud, and Siegmund Weiss. After graduating from the University of Vienna Medical School, he was appointed head of a hospital for internal and neurological diseases in Graz. Two years later, at the age of 30, he was named Assistant Director of a hospital for psychiatry and drug addiction in Reckawinkel, near Vienna. At the beginning of World War II, he moved to the United States and set up a private practice in New York City, where he specialized in internal and psychosomatic medicine.

As do all true healers, Franz Winkler probed for the root cause of each patient's illness—illnesses that he often saw as a reflection of conflicts besetting mankind as a whole. Through personal observation and experience he verified to his own satisfaction that most of the maladies of our time, whether individual or endemic, stem from an impairment of man's vision of himself. Such vision, or lack thereof, lames man's ability to direct his thoughts and actions rightly in meeting life's challenges.

Few men of our epoch achieve as much insight into the whole man as Franz Winkler did, and even fewer have helped so many others to orient themselves in today's complex world. In his lectures and writings, he frequently prescribed the study of myths and legends as one of the most effective ways of gaining a true picture of the human self. In the following chapters, Winkler clearly demonstrates what instruction and inspiration can be found in these time-honored sagas. With probity and daring, he dives into the heart of Wagner's meaning and finds the essential clue to what Wagner, and the legends that he used, were trying to reveal about the mystery of man's high origin and lofty goal.

Wagner's Artistic Ideal

An Introductory Comment

Many music historians, critics, and commentators have tried to tie Wagner's dramas of the Ring to his political and social activities of the 1840's. There are, no doubt, analogies between the legends Wagner used and the outer conditions of life in his day. The legends would not be the treasures they are if they were not applicable to most periods of history—if one could not see in them the ever-renewed struggle between good and evil that is reflected in the significant events of past and present time. Similarly, Wagner's operas would still be major works of art if they were mere allegories of his own era, but their true greatness lies in the universality and timelessness of their musical and poetic content.

It is true that in *Art and Revolution* and *The Artwork of the Future,* Wagner emphasizes how desirable it is that art have a timely and social significance; and this thesis apparently has been taken to mean that his principal motive for choosing myths and legends for his librettos was their allegoric reference to the social evils of Germany in the mid-nineteenth century. But the operas themselves, and the majority of his other writings, show that he intended to go far beyond any economic or political concern of his day. In 1847, for example, the year in which he was perhaps the most outspoken in his political views, he completed *Lohengrin,* an opera that can hardly be viewed as of primarily economic and political significance. And the poetic basis for the Ring cycle, the *Death of Siegfried,* had been started several years earlier when he was much less engaged in political polemics than he later became.

For Wagner, the purpose of art was to set a mirror before man so that he could see the reflection of his inner self, as well as his place in the universe. It was with this in mind that during his work on *Lohengrin,* he plunged into an extensive study of mythology. He began to see the myths as an artistic vehicle for a view of the truly human, and he wrote of his discovery:

> In the struggle to give the wishes of my heart artistic shape, and in the ardour to discover *what* thing it was that drew me so irresistibly to the primal source of old home Sagas, I drove step by step into the deeper regions of antiquity, where at last to my delight, and truly in the *utmost* reaches of old time, I was to light upon the fair young form of *Man,* in all the freshness of his force. My studies thus bore me, through the legends of the Middle Ages, right down to their foundation in the old Germanic Mythos; one swathing after another, which the later legendary lore had bound around it, I was able to unloose, and thus at last to gaze upon it in its chastest beauty. What here I saw was no longer the Figure of conventional history, whose garment claims our interest more than does the actual shape inside; but the real naked Man, in whom I might spy each throbbing of his pulse, each stir within his mighty muscles, in un-cramped, freest motion: the type of the true *human* being.[1]

Wagner continued to search for the right source for his art, a source that would also lead the spectator to a fuller understanding of the highest aspects of his own individuality. He deliberated between myth and conventional history, and finally chose myth, because it deals with primal causes and the inner man, whereas history treats of outer relationships.

> Myth and History stood before me with opposing claims,...forcing me to decide whether it was a musical drama, or a spoken play, that I had to write.[2]

> I felt that the highest of what I had seen from the
> purely human standpoint, and longed to show to
> others, could not be imparted in the treatment of a
> historico-political subject; that the mere intellectual
> *exposition of relations* made it impossible for me to
> present the purely human Individuality.[3]
> ...
>
> I had the most urgent occasion to clear my mind as to
> the essential difference between the historico-
> political and the purely-human life; and when I
> knowingly and willingly gave up *Friedrich Bar-
> barossa* in which I had approached the closest to
> that political life, and...gave preference to the
> *Siegfried*, I had entered a new and most decisive
> period of my evolution, both as artist and as man: the
> period of *conscious artistic will* to continue on an
> altogether novel path, which I had struck with un-
> conscious necessity, and whereon I now, as man and
> artist, press on to meet a newer world.[4]

When one considers that writing the four Ring operas required twenty-six years, it becomes increasingly evident that
Wagner's political activities during the late 1840's could not
have been his primary motivation for the colossal work. Indeed,
in later years, though significantly prior to the operas' completion, he repudiated most of his earlier political and social
credos.

There is also reason to believe that Wagner's inspiration for
the Ring operas was so enormous that it lay in part beyond his
everyday consciousness. He felt at times that the work had a
will and life of its own. After realizing that the *Death of
Siegfried*, which in the finished work came to be called *The
Twilight of the Gods*, would have to be preceded by the story of
the young Siegfried, he wrote his friend, Franz Liszt, of the
fantastically impractical shape his music dramas were taking.
He had just conceived the final design for the Ring, which called
for writing two new works: *The Rhinegold* was to serve as a
prelude, and *The Valkyries* would provide the necessary

background for *Siegfried*. Wagner explained to Liszt that these additional parts of the music drama were not calculated, but had arisen from the demands of the work itself. In answering, Liszt reminded his friend of the directions given by the Chapter of Seville to the architect of its new cathedral: "Build for us such a temple that future generations will say that the Chapter was crazy to undertake anything so extraordinary."[5]

In spite of his imaginative and grandiose ideas, Wagner was fully acquainted with the practical limitations of the theater of his day. He proceeded with his great work like a man who could not stop, although he must have been aware that his creation was virtually impossible to perform in any existing opera house. He wrote, in fact, that he doubted that the Ring could ever be produced. He had written his *Death of Siegfried,* he said, only as a kind of consolation for the disgust he had long felt for modern life and modern art. Still, he dreamt of the opera's performance and hoped he could recreate a religious festival like those for which the Greek tragedies were written, "where the gods bestirred themselves upon the stage and bestowed on men their wisdom."[6]

> Just as I had won a solid anchorage for the character of my dramatico-musical ideal in the rare and isolated doings of brilliant artists, so history supplied me with a typical model for that ideal relation, dreamt by me, of Theatre and Public. I found it in the theatre of ancient Athens, where its walls were thrown open on none but special, sacred feast-days, where the taste of Art was coupled with the celebration of a religious rite in which the most illustrious members of the State themselves took part as poets and performers, to appear like priests before the assembled populace of field and city; a populace filled with such high awaitings from the sublimeness of the artwork to be set before it that a Sophocles, an Aeschylus, could set before the Folk the deepest meaning of all poems, assured of their understanding.[7]
>
> ...

This people, streaming in its thousands from the State-assembly, from the Agore, from land, from sea, from camps, from distant parts,—filled with its thirty thousand heads the amphitheatre. To see the most pregnant of all tragedies, the *Prometheus*, came they; in this Titanic masterpiece to see the image of themselves, to read the riddle of their own actions, to fuse their own being and their own communion with that of their god; and thus in noblest, stillest peace to live again the life, which a brief space of time before, they had lived in restless activity and accentuated individuality.[8]

So convinced was Wagner of the revelatory effect his music dramas could and should have on the spectator that he conceived his plan for the Festspielhaus at Bayreuth. There the four Ring operas were to be produced on four successive evenings, before an audience especially gathered for the occasion. His detailed instructions for the interior, backstage, and orchestra pit, not to mention his stage directions, show his intention of producing an atmosphere in which music, words, and visual elements would speak to the heart, inducing a kind of "initiation" in those who came with an open mind. Referring to *Parsifal*, which he also intended for Bayreuth, Wagner wrote that it would be an outrage "like the profanation of the Eleusinian mysteries" if this work, "in which the sublimest mysteries of the Christian faith are shown upon the stage," were to be produced in the public theater of Germany, with its usual "late-comings and early-goings, its chatter, its boredom, and all the rest of it."[9] It was, he claimed, in "full consciousness of this that I gave *Parsifal* the description of a 'stage dedication play.' I must have for it, therefore, a dedicated stage, and this can only be my theatre in Bayreuth."[10]

Of course, one can view Alberich wielding a master's whip over the helpless Nibelungs at work in the dark mine shafts as a sombre, frightening allegory of the slaves of capitalism or the sweatshop laborers of industry. But this is to interpret the work narrowly and at the same time superficially. Wagner was far more concerned with preserving and quickening in all men an awareness of their destiny. Such awareness can doubtless shed light on the changing riddles of society, but only if it is founded in the unchanging realities of the human spirit.

If there is one theme in Wagner's operas that overshadows any other, it is the mystery of love; above all, the fateful choice that faces man: Will he renounce love for the sake of power, or will he seek redemption through a love that renounces self-seeking?

When Wagner began his great work, he had no idea how far he would have to go before he could resolve the question implicit in the myths and legends upon which he drew. He recognized in the German consciousness, as reflected in the Germanic poets of the Middle Ages, that the symbolic Nibelung hoard had yielded to a higher spiritual reality—the Grail. The legend of the Holy Grail had inspired Wagner to write *Lohengrin*. Now he felt compelled to return to it, in order to trace how the divine substance represented in the Ring cycle by the Rhinegold had become the receptacle of divine love that later appeared to man in the form of the Holy Grail.

The quest for the Grail, as set before us in *Parsifal*, brings man's evolutionary search for the secret of his own identity and his true goal in life right up to the present. It poses the crucial challenge that will determine the individual, social and ecological future. When rightly understood, this quest reveals to man that in the deeper consciousness of his soul he must kindle warmth and enthusiasm for his role on earth as a being of spirit, the servant and redeemer of nature rather than its exploiter. It requires him to see in himself Amfortas, as well as Parsifal. This last and greatest of Wagner's operas calls upon modern man to overcome apathy and doubt, and to commit himself to the service of the good. As Franz Winkler points out, there is more than a hint in *Parsifal* that if the men of today can rise above the narrow scientific thinking that now confuses and confines the human spirit, they can find truly creative solutions to the problems and sickness of our civilization. They may tap the source from which Wagner drew; for as Wagner once remarked to a friend, "I am convinced that there are universal currents of Divine Thought, and that anyone who can feel these vibrations is inspired, provided he is conscious of the process and possesses the knowledge and skill to realize them."[11]

M. G. H. Gilliam

Chapter I

THE MYTHOLOGY IN WAGNER'S RHINEGOLD

Most of the librettos of Richard Wagner's operas contain a wisdom never fully appreciated by an era dedicated to the purely intellectual approach to cognition. Today Wagner, philosopher, poet, and seer, is even less known than during his lifetime. In the United States, his works are rarely performed, and while many opera lovers still know and cherish his great compositions, they too pay scant attention to the treasure of myths and legends from which he drew. This is not surprising, since his operas are sung in German, and their official translations are extremely inadequate. Summaries available in programs and textbooks are apt to leave in the reader an impression of turgid Germanic mysticism and of a dream world unrelated to real life. Even in German-speaking countries, little understanding remains of Wagner's message. This may be due partly to the difficulties his alliterative language poses, partly to Germans themselves, and partly to the unpleasant memory of the attempt

Hitler and his clique made to appropriate Germanic mythology for the furthering of their aims.

Wagner's defenders, who share neither the antagonism nor the contempt for his librettos, are likely to point out that great composers have often taken the liberty of using rather inferior plots, without detriment to their artistic mission. Why then should Wagner be blamed for cultivating a dream world of his own, so long as this world provides a colorful background for his great music? Defense of this kind, however, disregards a basic fact. Whoever studies the composer's letters, theoretical writings, and personal notes must realize that Wagner's main purpose in life was to give a message to the world rather than merely to write opera. His great music was, for him, not an end in itself but merely part of a vision that he considered a divine gift to the world. This is the reason why he risked his reputation as a composer by writing his own librettos, and why he wanted his works known as music dramas rather than operas, seeking to have them performed under conditions conducive to a spiritual experience.

Wagner did not stand alone in his attempt to warn the world that a purely intellectual approach to cognition leads to disaster. Before him, no less a person than Goethe risked his tremendous prestige by carrying the fight for a revival of intuitive faculties into the domain of science. The attitude of these two men was by no means anti-intellectual. They merely believed, as Emerson expressed it, that "at present, man applies to nature but half his forces;... and he that works most in it is but a half-man."[12]

In epochs preceding our modern scientific age, there existed an intuitive comprehension of natural phenomena, a comprehension revealed in the emergence of the great

religions as well as in immortal art. There was then relatively little scientific knowledge in the modern sense of
the word, so that for those times also it can be said that
man applied only one half of his being to the cognition
of truth. At that time it was the now almost forgotten
intuitive half. For only he applies his *whole* being who
makes use of both his intuitive and his intellectual faculties. The modern physicist knows a great deal about the
phenomena of light, but comprehension of its true nature
requires an intuitive experience such as that revealed by
Rembrandt and other masters of light.

The intuitive aspect of cognition is frequently ridi-
culed today for its fallibility. This fallibility, however,
has not always existed, as any conscientious student of
the history of science can easily discover. For all truly
creative scientists have credited their discoveries to intuitive experiences at least as much as to intellectual activity.
The unreliability of intuition today is only the inevitable
result of disuse. Just as a man who has been confined to
complete darkness for a very long time, and is returned to
light again, will encounter great difficulties in correctly
evaluating optical phenomena, so modern man needs
patient training toward the redevelopment of inner vision,
which has gone unused during centuries devoted to an
outward-oriented, intellectual activity. Without this vision,
the Bible states, "the people perish."

Every phenomenon has two roots, one accessible
to sense perception and intellectual investigation, the
other to intuitive and artistic experience. If we can see
only one of them, and try to find full reality through a
half-experience, we fall victim to illusion and superstition; and if we persist in acting as "half-men," we may
actually destroy nature and ourselves. Confronted with

another human being, we cannot possibly hope to understand him if we restrict ourselves to his physical nature
and to a purely scientific point of view. Mentally we may
take him apart organ by organ, and even cell by cell,
without ever finding a trace of that real and existing self
with which alone we can deal in friendship, love, and
understanding. Yet when we think of the origin of man,
we insist illogically on confusing the history of his purely
biological being with the history of his spirit; the latter
defies any attempt at investigation by methods we now
call scientific. Darwin and his followers deal with the
emergent evolution of visible man, while on the other
hand, religion and mythology deal with the evolution of
his invisible soul. In the cycle of the Ring, Richard Wagner
uses the magic power of music, words, and scenery to
open man's heart to the history of the hidden essence of
his own self, and to the changing forces that are active
behind the sensory phenomena of man and earth.

The *Ring of the Nibelung* is the saga not only of individual man, but also of God's supreme gift to the world:
the gift that endows its rightful owner with the power to
recreate and transform the earth. The alchemists called
it the philosophers' stone, early Christian mystics, the
Holy Grail. Wagner termed its pre-Christian manifestation
the Rhinegold.

In the first opera of the Ring tetralogy, the creative
power of the Rhinegold is entrusted to the watery element,
the element from which all life has sprung. The curtain
rises on a scene beneath the surface of the Rhine. Guarded
by the river's daughters, the Rhinegold lies asleep. This
tale of the earth does not start with man, but with the
elements of which the planet is composed. Since time
immemorial, these prime components have been sought
in water, fire, air and solid earth. Naturally, when myth-

ology speaks of these principles it does not refer to their physical manifestations alone, but to the wisdom and power behind them that establish their laws. To the intuitive perception which modern thinking has almost entirely lost, the essence of the elements appeared in living images familiar to folklore all over the world. Wagner leaves no doubt that the first scene of his *Rhinegold* takes place in such a causative world, hidden within or behind the element of water from which life originally emerged. The "Father" himself has withdrawn from his creation, but he has left behind "an eye of gold" which can still behold the master plan of that creation. An epoch has come to an end, an epoch called by the Bible the Garden of Eden, by the Indians Krita Yuga, and by the Greeks the Age of Gold. A new era is dawning, carrying in itself the seeds of freedom. Discontent and the struggle for domination of the earth begins.

No longer are the elements content with their appointed part in creation. The restlessness of a changing planet is dramatically revealed by the appearance of Alberich, the dwarf. He represents the element of solid earth, just as the Rhine Maidens represent the fluid element of water. Alberich is driven by his longing toward lighter worlds, by an urge to leave his own task in the depths of the earth unfinished and to join, prematurely, an existence of a higher order. As in all myths, his passionate longing is described in an anthropomorphic way. It is described as lust for beings of another order. Beings without physical bodies do not know eroticism in the human sense, but they can attract or repel one another. Their union even creates offspring, resulting in new impulses and, as the alchemists claimed, in the appearance of new substances or mutations within the world of chemistry and biology.

Since most beings strive from darkness towards light, the Rhine Maidens appear desirable to the son of darkness. But for the same reason he and his kind seem repulsive to them. Alberich's suit is rejected in mockery and contempt, until eventually his passionate desire turns into cold hatred.

The sun is rising and its rays reveal the priceless treasure of the Rhine in all its unearthly beauty. Alberich's attention is now caught by a light far brighter than the glittering of the watery element itself. He inquires after the meaning of the treasure, and is only too willingly enlightened by its devout admirers.

This is not gold as it exists in the rivers and bowels of the earth, but the archetype of gold. It represents forces of highest value to the earth, forces which, if used for selfish ends, may give their owner an almost unlimited power. Yet the Rhine Maidens are not afraid that Alberich will avail himself of such power, for only he who forswears love entirely can obtain and use it. They do not realize that their cruel rejection has already extinguished his hope for love. Now he is willing to curse love and thus to turn God's gift into a selfish means for power and destruction.

> *Your light I extinguish;*
> *I wrest from the rock the gold*
> *To fashion for vengeance the Ring!*
> *For hear me, O flood —*
> *Love I curse now, forever.*

With the awakening of self-consciousness, the Rhine-gold passes into the hands of Alberich, the representative of the hardening, solidifying forces in life. To attain god-like power, Alberich breaks allegiance to his creator by

forswearing the one bond that connects him with all creatures, the bond of love. Forging the Rhinegold into a ring,
the ancient symbol of selfhood, Alberich emerges as the
prince of darkness, the representative of those forces on
earth which ever try to turn God's gift into a tool of self-
ishness and hate.

Precious metals have always played a significant
part in mythology and folklore. It is not the substance
itself, but its archetype, that is meaningful to the myth.
From earliest times, religious experience in its highest
form has led to the intuitive vision of a golden light. Gold
itself represented only the physical counterpart of such
an experience. Consequently, it served primarily ritual
purposes; it was used to fashion golden images of gods
and, later, golden halos of saints. This explains the almost
magic effect that the precious metal created, as inner
vision faded and man's unfulfilled longing for the divine
became directed to its material reflection. This may
account for the fact that gold, though in itself of little
practical use, came eventually to be valued beyond reason
and coveted with a greed bordering on obsession, a greed
that drove mankind to some of its basest exploits. For in
the last analysis, it is not material gain that causes the
strongest passions in man, but longing for spiritual values.
This longing comes to be misdirected and misunderstood
by men who lose their vision.

Why is it that only he who renounces love — and with
it God, for God is love — can attain the power of consci-
ously misusing divine gifts? It is because, as some of the
greatest medieval mystics and philosophers taught, God
could not have given freedom to any of His creatures
had he not left them some of His own essence to use as
they would. This divine essence has been misused over
and over again by man in his trials and errors, but he

who has preserved so much as a trace of love hidden somewhere in his heart cannot turn wholly against God, even when he believes he does. He, however, who would actually forswear and curse love in full consciousness of his act, may take hold of creative forces for his own egotistical aims, assume within his own sphere of influence divine prerogatives, and bring terrible suffering to his fellow-creatures.

Whereas the first scene of Wagner's *Rhinegold* took us into the twilight zone of the watery element, the second takes us into the lofty sphere of air and light. The beings residing there were called by various peoples the upper gods, *Lichtalben*, or sylphs. Their leader in German mythology was Wotan, who ruled the world as protector of just treaties and equal rights. Sun and air bestow their gifts on all creatures alike. The lightning that strikes, the storm that destroys, know no favorite. Thus a certain equality existed, and its existence was credited to the upper gods, the bringers of light into the darkness of blind rule by power. But the world was changing, and even the god, Wotan, dreamed of power for its own sake. In order to perpetuate the supremacy of the upper gods and their rule, he desired a castle in lofty heights, a fortress far removed from the other creatures of the earth. He himself did not have the power to build it; thus he bargained with the giants to do it for him.

The giants in Wagner's mythology are representatives of primordial man. They are "the race that lives on the back of the earth," just as the gods dwell in its heights and the dwarfs or gnomes in its depths. Wagner casts the giants to appear in the shape of primitive man: their minds simple but already cunning, and their instinctive strength, not yet channeled to intellectual pursuits, gigantic. Originally the pagan gods ruled men only by virtue of their greater wisdom. Only man could build for them invisible fortresses, fortresses in the form of creeds that in later times would close out the living experience of the gods from mankind and enable some men to rule in the gods' stead by fear. Yet it is an illusion of modern materialism that the gods were mere figments of the human mind. As indicated earlier, primitive man still experienced "intelligences" living between heaven and earth. These "intelligences" could misuse their power just as a human being can misuse his. Wotan needed man, whom the giants represent, to build his Valhalla, but they would do so only at a price. They demanded Freia, the goddess of spring, youth, and eternal renewal. Man in his primitive state did not mind erecting walls between himself and the gods, thus submitting himself to creeds that for thousands of years would make him a worshipper of pagan deities, but in return he wanted the rejuvenating power of nature, Freia, all for himself.

It seems that during those long, mysterious eras preceding the Neolithic Age, nature gave man all that he needed, without toil. But in his instincts the desire to rule nature may already have stirred. With the invention of agriculture and animal husbandry in the Neolithic "revolution," man indeed attained some control over regeneration and procreation in nature. Once these powers were securely in the hands of humans, the gods would wither and die. How then could Wotan have promised to hand Freia over to the giants? Because a new force had entered the vast stage of world evolution, the force of temptation and deceit.

In Wagner's opera it is Loge who persuades Wotan to make a promise he does not intend to fulfill. Loge was the god of the fiery element. For ancient consciousness, the later conflict between monism and dualism did not exist. Just as the tangible body of man had an intangible soul, so was every element the sense-perceptible body of an intuitively experienced "intelligence." Raging fire was the physical counterpart of a restless spirit whose tendency is to destroy rather than to serve. According to ancient thinking, Loge had been conquered by Wotan. Hence, the lightning striking a dead tree, or the rays of the sun igniting dry tinder, appeared as a gift of the gods to man. In mastering the fire thus given, man tamed and controlled the power of destruction. But fire eternally longs to break free, and thus its genius wants to bring discord between gods and man so that in the ensuing chaos it can ravish the earth and the dwelling place of the gods. Loge knows that Wotan is not permitted to fulfill his promise to hand over the secrets of life, personified by Freia, to primitive man. And thus he suggests a substitute, potentially even more dangerous in the hands of man — the hoard of the Nibelung.

The Nibelung hoard is the material treasure harvested from seed sown by greed. The spirit gold of the Rhine Maidens, stolen by Alberich and fashioned into the Ring, gave its owner undisputed power over Nibelhome, the subterranean kingdom in which he dwelt, and over its vast mineral resources. Thus Alberich compels the Nibelung dwarfs to amass a hoard that will eventually ensure his rule of the planet. The hoard's greatest treasure is the tarnhelm, or helmet, an object containing the power to transform the appearance of its wearer. The legend touches here a phenomenon that the modern mind is loath to accept. It is the phenomenon of magic, whose existence in ancient times, as well as among primitive peoples of today, has been reported a thousand times but seems to have disappeared almost totally so far as our present state of consciousness is concerned. Actually, it has only been transformed into modern technology, which would have appeared to our ancestors as the greatest of all magic feats. The spiritual force of modern man flows into matter by way of intellectual reasoning, while in earlier epochs it took the more direct path of a sheer exertion of will power. Just as by applied science we are able to exert power and change material forms, Alberich, still close to the workshop of nature itself, used magic to transform his physical appearance.

One of man's evolutionary aims is to develop a clearly defined individuality while using his powers of transformation for the good of the world. When Alberich undertakes to change his shape into any form he chooses, but for selfish purposes, he reverses the trend of evolution. The pride with which he displays this magic faculty becomes his undoing. Wotan and Loge, counting on this weakness of pride, persuade the dwarf to disguise himself in the likeness of a toad. Taking advantage of his momentary helplessness, they seize and compel him to part not only with his treasures but also with his power of transformation as symbolized by the helmet that the magic of the Ring had enabled him to create.

From this scene until the end of the whole cycle, Alberich's Ring remains the mysterious power behind the evolving tragedy. Many a modern critic has scoffed at Wagner's use of inanimate objects as causative factors in dramatic events. What these critics forget, however, is the relatively minor part the conscious mind plays in the shaping of history even today, not to mention epochs when individual consciousness was much weaker than it is now. Nor, for that matter, is the Nibelung's Ring an inanimate object. It symbolizes a spiritual force that is being used before the world is ripe for it. Alberich has fashioned the Rhinegold into an archetypal symbol that appears in the folklore of almost all peoples. The Ring is an object that takes the contemplating mind on an unending journey around the finger it adorns. Where it is extended into the symbolic hoop, which played a significant part in the tribal life of American Indians, it signifies abandonment of *individual* selfhood to the selfhood of the tribe. Where it is exchanged, as in modern wedding rites, it symbolizes a degree of mutual sacrifice of the self for the sake of love.

Alberich has no intention of sharing. Nor does he develop his individuality by moral efforts, but rather by excluding himself from all the currents of sympathy and love that normally bind one being to another. This separation from a more inclusive consciousness, attained by forswearing love, singles him out while at the same time it endows him with unique power. He is forced to abandon this power only when, blinded by pride, he transforms himself momentarily into the guise of a defenseless creature. Wotan, however, by his trickery unwittingly dooms himself. He who had hitherto ruled by virtue of just treaties has now broken his own laws. Undoubtedly, Alberich, a thief himself, had no moral right to possession of the Ring. Yet to attain it, he had made a terrible sacrifice — he had forsworn love forever. This sacrifice gave him lasting power over the Ring, an evil power that he uses to bestow a curse of doom upon its new and undeserving possessor. One might even say that it is the same curse that rests, to our day, on all selfhood that goes unredeemed by purity and love.

Soon after Wotan has robbed Alberich of his treasure, he again must face the two giants, Fafner and Fasolt, representatives of the pre-intellectual human race. The price for building Valhalla, the fortress of the gods, had been Freia, the goddess of youth and rejuvenation. Spurred by a newly developing greed for gold, the giants are persuaded to exchange her for the Nibelung hoard, but their condition is that the gold be piled to such a height and width that it hides completely from their view the vision of the lovely goddess.

This demand reveals a far-reaching psychological truth. Man loves the beauty of nature and wants to use its bounty for his own enjoyment. But his greed for gold may be so great as to dazzle him, making him forget the greater values of life. Is he not to our day ready to forsake and even to despoil the beauty of his planet, and indeed the cosmos, in fulfillment of this greed? Wotan, on the other hand, is only too willing to part with the material gold dug by the dwarfs from the bowels of the earth. He believes that the giants will content themselves with it without demanding the only possession he really covets, the Ring. But, as mentioned earlier, man's greed for material values, especially for the glittering gold, is tenacious precisely for the reason that it represents, in the last analysis, a misguided longing for spiritual treasures.

The Nibelung hoard piled in front of Freia can hide her image, but it cannot blot out the shine of her golden hair nor the radiant "star of her eye." In legend and myth the hair denotes something of significance. It denotes spiritual power, just as the eye symbolizes spiritual vision. When Samson has lost his purity, his hair is shorn and his eyes are destroyed. The spiritual leader succumbing to temptation loses the power and vision of his soul. Only through suffering can he regain his spiritual strength (when his hair grows long again) and destroy the temple of the idols. Thus it should come as no surprise when, in the unerring logic of his intuitive wisdom, Wagner tells us that the giants could not be satisfied with their exchange of Freia for gold until not only her image but even the memory of her hair and eyes had been extinguished. To blot out the hair, primitive man required the power of magic, for magic is a decadent manifestation of spiritual strength. The symbol of magic power in the opera is the magic helmet. To forget her eye, the vision of the divine, the giants require the Ring of the Nibelung, which represents not physical gold but the last vestige on earth of universal spiritual vision.

Wotan refuses to part with the Ring until an image arises before him, the image of a being whose knowledge and power are greater than his own. For the first time he becomes aware of a wisdom germane to the planet itself. For the earth is not merely a gigantic ball born of and sustained by blind mechanical forces, existing just for the pleasure of the self-seeking race of man. It is a living entity endowed with an unfathomable wisdom of its own. The Greeks called the soul of the earth Gaea. In antiquity, she was worshipped in the Uroboric Mysteries, and in more modern times, the spirit of the earth appears in Goethe's *Faust* in masculine form. Wagner sees this spirit as the "Earth Mother" Erda. Erda's universal wisdom far exceeds the partial one of the elements of light and air, as personified in Wotan, and she can therefore admonish him:

> *Whatever has been . . . I know,*
> *Whatever is to be, whatever will come,*
> *I see it clearly.*
> *The eternal soul of this world,*
> *Erda, . . . gives you warning . . .*
> *Flee the curse of . . . the Ring,*
> *Its possession will seal your doom!*

Wotan heeds Erda's warning and yields the Ring to the

giants, but a new longing arises in him: the longing to fathom the aim of creation.

The giants Fafner and Fasolt are now in possession of the Nibelung treasure, but their primitive minds and hearts do not know how to use it. And Alberich's curse strikes like lightning. In the attempt to share their reward, they confront an unsolvable problem. For the Ring *cannot* be shared. It is a spiritual power far beyond the comprehension of aboriginal man, a power that has been prematurely fashioned into the symbol of selfhood. And selfhood cannot be shared. It takes but little support from Loge, the tempter, to kindle greed into hate and hate into murder. Morally and spiritually unready for the Ring, brother turns against brother and commits the first crime, fratricide. Fafner slays Fasolt and carries away the hoard. Incapable of using it for the good of the world but unwilling to part with it, Fafner turns into a monster and merely "lies and possesses."

Fateful events of evolution are re-enacted in various forms and on various levels, time and again. Thus it is not surprising that this fratricide bears a resemblance to Cain's murder of Abel. Cain and Abel represent mankind in the stage of evolution after the consciousness of the Garden of Eden, the Age of Gold, has faded. Cain kills Abel in envy. For Abel has still retained some of man's original vision of God. In a much cruder form, Fafner's slaying of Fasolt mirrors the Biblical event. For Fafner kills Fasolt not only out of greed, but also because he cannot forgive his brother for having preferred the divine beauty of Freia to the possession of the gold.

And thus begins a new era of consciousness. The gods withdraw from the earth to a "lofty castle" built by man himself. Although man now owns all that could make him the ruler of his earth, for a long time to come he will know only how to possess what he can neither use nor enjoy. Unheeded by god and man alike, rises the lament of the Rhine Maidens:

> *Rhinegold, Rhinegold, purest gold,*
> *O would thy light still glow in the deep!*
> *Purity and faithfulness abide only with us;*
> *What preens itself in the heights is*
>   *fearful and false.*

The curtain falls on the first act of a cosmic drama, the drama of evolution, which does not concern the human race alone but all creatures, gods and men alike. The innocent childhood of the gods has ended. Wotan has broken the laws that he had pledged to uphold, the laws that protect the sanctity of the given word. The Guardian of Treaties never meant to keep the promise that he made to the giants. Even worse, he had obtained the hoard of the Nibelung from the dwarf by trickery. Now, confronted with the existence of a wisdom greater than his own, he abandons his gain and takes, albeit unwittingly, the first step on the long journey of evolution, a journey of atonement that must eventually end in the doom of the gods.

Chapter II

THE MYTHOLOGY IN WAGNER'S VALKYRIE

One of the major obstacles on the path to a better world is man's misconception of himself. Popular misinterpretation of Darwin's great discoveries and naive acceptance of the Freudian obsession with sex threaten to undermine the very foundation of self-knowledge and, with it, any clear understanding of the meaning of life. The adult, resigned to and supported by the manifold duties of daily life, may well plod along without the incentive of a higher goal. Not so, young people. For many of them, life appears so meaningless that every form of learning and obedience to their elders seems a wasted effort. Thus without the comprehension of its purpose, without a goal to strive for, life is for many young people unbearably dull.

This lack of motivation stems basically from man's materialistic concept of himself. If his innermost nature *were* merely biological, complete fulfillment of his appetites and the acquiring of wealth would satisfy his longing for happiness. Since they do not, an atmosphere of hopelessness is enveloping our generation, especially our youth. In an affluent society where all material ways out of such frustration have been found wanting, drugs, perversities, and the thrills of crime are now being used as desperate means of escape from the intolerable boredom. Well-meaning efforts on the part of the authorities to stem the tidal wave of juvenile delinquency and drug addiction will therefore bring scant results, until the following simple truth has been fully accepted by parents and teachers.

Happiness, love, and compassion are spiritual faculties that during centuries of neglect and misunderstanding have withered and grown weak. Unless they are nursed back to health, man will despair of life and eventually throw it away in a mass suicide by nuclear destruction. But how can we care for what we no longer comprehend? Modern science, admirable in its achievements on a material plane, has proven ineffectual in the understanding of intangible values. This limitation, while freely admitted by the small number of truly creative scientists, seems to elude the average intellectual. And the failure to recognize this limitation adds to the delusion that natural science in its present form can be the judge of religious or spiritual truth.

Making modern man's plight even more serious is the fact that his materialistic delusion of himself not only deprives him of wisdom and happiness, but it acts also as a pattern in whose dreary image he tends to reshape his nature. Consequently, more and more personalities emerge who think and act virtually like robots. They know no happiness, and have no perception of objective morality. The distorted concept that modern man has formed of himself leaves him defenseless against the fantastic prophecies made in popular articles dealing with progress in biology. We are told that a human breed may be raised by stimulating ovulation or multiplying the traits of a specific individual from tissue growth. Ever since such prospects have become known to the public, the agonized question has been heard: "But where can the human soul be found in all these artifacts?" Well, where in a player-piano can the piano player be found?

We have grown wise in the analysis of the material world, have expanded the scope of our perception to outer space and to the world beneath the atom. But objective *inner* experience has faded almost entirely away, and it has left us groping in the dark for the true image of ourselves. Since the beginning of history, the great leaders of mankind have tried to bring light into the gathering darkness of man's life on earth. Moses, Buddha, Jesus, Plato, Aristotle, Goethe, and Emerson are just a few of them. As a human being, Richard Wagner with his glaring shortcomings of character may not fit into that illustrious group. Yet in moments of artistic inspiration, a wellspring must have opened in the soul of that strange magician, from which undoubtedly flows a wealth of long-forgotten truth, and a kind of music that can reopen the gateways of spiritual perception.

At the end of the *Rhinegold*, Wotan took the Ring from Alberich by stealth and thus recklessly destroyed the very foundation on which his own dominion was built. The king of the gods, who in the age of paganism was worshipped as the protector of just laws and sacred treaties, transgressed his own principles. Warned by Erda, the spirit of the earth, that even he cannot escape the curse Alberich has laid on the Ring, Wotan reluctantly yielded it to the giants.

Wotan now knows that his own failure has deprived

him of the right to recover the treasure. Matured by the growing awareness of his guilt, he no longer desires its fateful power for himself, but he wants it to be the heritage of a breed of men nobler than the giant-turned-dragon who now possesses it. For Wotan knows only too well that Alberich will never relent in seeking the treasure for which he has paid with his soul. And Alberich, by forswearing love in his lust for power would turn life on earth into a nightmare of unspeakable horror. Should he regain the Ring, not even the gods could wrest it from him again or escape his wrath: men would be slaves, the beauty of the earth destroyed, her clear streams polluted, and the air befouled, until all life would cease. And for this Wotan would have to bear part of the guilt.

For long periods at a time the god leaves Valhalla, the castle for which he had paid so high a price, and becomes a fear-and-guilt-ridden wanderer in the world. Yet wherever he goes, new impulses arise, bringing about higher forms of consciousness. As symbolically expressed in the myth, he even embraces the Great Mother Earth, and out of that union spring nine daughters, the Valkyries. The most beloved by Wotan, Brunnhilde, is the first born. Their mission is to gather the souls of heroes fallen in a worthy cause, in order to fight evil in the world of the dead. Such souls were worshipped in older times as the Ancestors, the protectors of all that is good and sacred on earth. But Wotan knows that neither the living nor the dead can defy Alberich, once he has regained the Ring of power. To forestall this tragedy, Wotan's aim is to bring wisdom, courage, and especially freedom to the still lowly race of men, so that they will claim for themselves the power Alberich craves. In the language of mythology, Wotan marries a mortal and sires two children, Siegmund and Sieglinde.

Three archetypes of humanity now populate the world. Primitive tribes, still endowed with the magic forces of childhood but with no desire for change, are represented by the giant, Fafner.

Then there is average man, warlike and proud, selfish and cruel. Hunding, the lord of the manor in whose hall the first act of the *Valkyrie* takes place, is its chief representative. He has bought Sieglinde from brigands who, in the absence of her father and brother, have laid siege to their stronghold and carried her off. Neither asking nor offering love, Hunding takes her for his wife and holds her "prisoner" in his gloomy hall.

Sieglinde and her brother Siegmund, haunted by the enmity of lesser men who look with suspicion upon their superior development, represent the third breed. They are chosen by the god for bringing the impulse of freedom into the consciousness of man. Wotan leaves them to their ill fate, hoping that, unprotected, they will develop strength to become masters of their destiny and the founders of a noble race.

It was a fierce and proud generation of which the god dreamed, a generation that would wrest the Ring from its giant owner, turned dragon, defend it against Alberich, the prince of darkness, and with its divine power rule the world. The hearts of this new race would be living shrines for Wotan, their immortal father, whom they would serve in love and gratitude. Against such an alliance of wise gods and free men not even Alberich's curse and cunning could prevail. Yet while Wotan commits his children to the purifying ordeal of suffering, to give them the gift of freedom he plots their fate for them. Appearing as an unbidden guest at the wedding feast of Hunding and Sieglinde, he thrusts a sword into the trunk of an ancient tree, a sword that will yield to none but Siegmund in the hour of his greatest need.

This hour has now arrived, for Siegmund, wounded and unarmed, finds refuge in Hunding's house. Hunding is away from home, hunting the very man who unwittingly has sought shelter in his hall. The twins, Siegmund and Sieglinde, separated for many years, do not recognize each other, yet are irresistibly drawn together. A passion is kindled in their hearts that cannot be extinguished, even after they discover their kinship. When Hunding eventually returns, he has no choice but to respect the sanctuary granted to the guest by ancient law. But he warns the unarmed stranger that at break of dawn he will challenge him to mortal combat.

Sieglinde pours into her husband's mead a draught that sends him into deep sleep. Brother and sister, alone again, now plan their escape from Hunding's wrath, and Sieglinde shows Siegmund the sword buried to the hilt in the trunk of the tree. The weapon yields readily to the will of its appointed master. Armed with Needful, Siegmund fears no man alive. The heavy doors swing open as of their own accord, and moonlight floods Hunding's gloomy hall. The spring night adds its magic to Siegmund and Sieglinde's enchantment: heedless of the laws of gods and men, they yield to incestuous love.

If *Rhinegold* lifted us into a sphere high above the level of ordinary consciousness, the first act of the *Valkyrie* brings us right down to earth. In its second act the drama returns again to a higher plane, to the sphere of consciousness that is hidden from the hustle and bustle of ordinary life. The lovers have fled the hall of Hunding at the crack of dawn. Gone is the ecstasy of the night before, and in the all-encompassing silence of the mountain vastness their souls are wide open to the silent voices of the gods. Sieglinde feels the coming of doom, while Siegmund calmly awaits Hunding's wrath and the judgment of the gods. Though adultery and incest were crimes mercilessly punished according to the strict moral standards of Germanic tribes, his conscience is clear. Has not a power immeasurably greater than their own kindled an irresistible passion in brother and sister? And was not the sword waiting for him in Hunding's hall another sign of divine approval?

But not all the gods approve. Sieglinde's lawful husband has called on Fricka, the guardian of virtue and of marital vows, demanding punishment for Siegmund, whose offense not only destroyed Hunding's home but also threatens the very foundations of order and law. Fricka hears his prayer. Mounting a chariot drawn by rams, she rushes to Wotan, who has just ordered Brunnhilde to protect Siegmund in the battle to come.

The ram-drawn chariot is mentioned here to show that every detail in Wagner's original stage directions is meaningful. The archetypal image of the chariot, as for instance the one driven by Apollo in Greek mythology, indicates a heavenly body that in myth and ancient history stands invariably as an expression of cosmic wisdom. In the course of evolution, the various aspects of such divine guidance are thought to take turns directing the fate of men; their nature is implied by astrological signs. Thus the beginning of the Christian era was marked by the image of the fish, the zodiacal sign in which the sun still rises today at the spring equinox. The bull was worshipped in the Minoan-Cretan period, to be replaced by Aries, the ram, about 2000 years B.C. Consequently, the image of the ram became the guiding symbol of occidental culture after the decline of Cretan influence; it was remembered in the sacred relic of the Golden Fleece, and appeared on the helmets of Germanic warriors.

There are many more examples of the significance of the ram during the final era of paganism, all of which make it possible to interpret the ram-drawn chariot of Fricka as the sign of a cultural era that flourished and declined during the last two millennia before Christ. A new phase in the history of evolution will soon begin, a phase in which man, standing alone in freedom, will have to rule his destiny and build his own world. To succeed, he must learn to create his own moral standards without blind obedience to traditional laws. Fricka, however, knows nothing of the future. It is still her mission to protect the ancient order. True to it, she insists on punishment for the breaker of its laws.

The controversy that follows between Wotan and Fricka is often interpreted as a rather embarrassing quarrel between an unfaithful husband and his jealous wife. Conductors and stage directors are inclined to abbreviate the scene to the point where it loses all significance, though in fact it represents one of the most dramatic and meaningful events in literature. Wotan, posing as judge in Siegmund's indictment by Fricka, is in reality the defendant before the representative of the moral and spiritual order of the epoch. Grudgingly he defends himself by pointing to the crucial need for the emergence of free human beings, who might still turn the tide in the battle that the gods have lost. And how else can man achieve freedom if not by defying the ancient order and breaking its laws?

Fricka is unmoved. Mercilessly, she tears the veil from Wotan's eyes and exposes what he has not been able to admit to himself. In Siegmund's veins flows the blood of a god; he has shown great courage in trials surpassing the endurance of most mortals. Yet he is motivated by Wotan's will, not by his own, and thus remains unfree.

To understand the issue before the court of the gods, we must consider for a moment the pre-Christian concepts of man's relationship to destiny. Denial of a supersensible reality was almost unheard of before the fifth century B.C., for the simple reason that man's still-powerful intuitive perception left him no doubt as to its existence. People knew that their fate depended on higher powers, which they obeyed less from love given in freedom than from the compulsion of fear. "Honor thy father and mother, that thy days may be long upon the earth."

In the *Book of Job*, Jahve or Jehovah is challenged by Lucifer as to the very *possibility* of freedom. Man, so claims the prince of darkness, is loyal to God only because he seeks rewards and fears punishment. Put him to the test, and he will curse his creator and renounce the divine gift of life. Even Jahve cannot disregard this challenge, for if Lucifer were right, God's master plan of bringing into existence a free being would be based on error. Though by no means the only example in the Bible, the *Book of Job* is one of its most intriguing, in that it assigns to Jahve the part of the defendant, and to man that of judge and jury. Job, though subjected to suffering he has not deserved, and deprived of all accepted incentives for loyalty, acquits his creator by refusing to curse him and to renounce life. His faith in the law of just retribution shattered, his attitude toward God and destiny no longer determined by hope for reward or by fear of punishment, he nevertheless refuses to renounce God. Thus, as representative of the human race, he affirms man's potentiality for freedom and consents willingly to the aim of creation.

Jahve merely puts Job's *capacity* for freedom to the test; Wotan tries to *force* freedom on Siegmund. Moreover, his tests are far from conclusive, since it was Wotan who had brought brother and sister together, kindled their passion, put into Siegmund's hand the invincible sword, and finally ordered the Valkyrie to protect him in the battle with Hunding. If Siegmund's claim to freedom is to be founded on heroic deeds unaided by the gods, then — so Fricka challenges Wotan — deprive him of the invincible sword and let him face Hunding unaided by the Valkyrie!

At last Wotan concedes defeat. In a magnificent dialogue, he bares his heart to Brunnhilde, rescinds his command that she aid Siegmund, and orders her to bring about Siegmund's doom.

> . . . All my cunning could not conceal it,
> So easily Fricka found out the lie . . .
> Of no use is my will,
> For freedom cannot be willed.

From Brunnhilde Wotan keeps no secrets; is she not part of his own soul, the very echo of his heart? The story of his shattered hopes, failures, and humiliations reaches a climax in these words:

> In ruins may fall all I have built;
> I surrender my mission;
> One thing alone I crave: the end.

While his fate is being decided, Siegmund watches over Sieglinde, who at last has found peace in the merciful sleep of exhaustion. Trials, undeserved and almost beyond endurance, had been ordained for both by the god. Yet while the divine experiment has failed to give them freedom, it has implanted in their hearts a faculty virtually unknown to that era, the faculty of selfless love.

While Siegmund keeps silent watch, a vision takes

shape before his inner eye: Brunnhilde, the Valkyrie, reveals herself as was her custom to those destined to die. Resigned to his fate, he has only one request: to take Sieglinde along into the realm of the dead. Brunnhilde cannot fulfill this wish, for Sieglinde's hour has not yet come. But Siegmund will not leave his beloved alone in a hostile world. If the gods have forsaken her, he himself will set her free from the tribulations of the earth. The Valkyrie, stirred by compassion and knowing Sieglinde to be with child, stays his hand. In defiance of Wotan, she resolves to help Siegmund to victory in the ensuing battle with Hunding and to save Sieglinde and their unborn child.

An epoch is prematurely drawing to its end. A god had dreamed a dream and decided to make it come true. But freedom imposed on man is not freedom, and Siegmund, the innocent victim of a god's error, must die. Wotan has put into motion a process whose course he can no longer control, and Brunnhilde, his alter ego, "part of his soul, the very echo of his will," defies his command. She tries to save the hero's life and, had Wotan not interfered, would have succeeded. The god's spear shatters the mighty sword, Needful, and weaponless, Siegmund dies at Hunding's hand.

The third act carries the ancient order closer to its dissolution. The previous disagreements between Fricka, still a guardian of this order, and Wotan, the initiator of a new age, reflect no more than the inevitable conflicts between old and new impulses. The disobedience of his beloved Valkyrie daughter, however, presages Wotan's fall. Freedom cannot be given; it must be earned, and its price is high. The suffering the god imposed on his mortal children was not of their choosing, and it therefore failed to achieve its immediate purpose. The pain Wotan suffered himself, however, has led the world closer to the realization of his dream. To achieve this realization, divine power had to decrease; and it did weaken, by setting one part of the god's soul against the other. There is no longer room for Brunnhilde in the realm of the gods; only among men can she fulfill her mission.

Wotan's wish is to be granted at the very time when all hope for its fulfillment has been lost. In the offspring of Siegmund and Sieglinde the world will know its first free man. But new impulses in the evolution of the conscious mind always appear in a twofold aspect: the male and the female. Siegfried, representing the male aspect, will be able to conceive ideas unfettered by ancient tradition. Still, what the masculine mind creates must be fructified by the warmth of feminine intuition and feminine love. Brunnhilde is destined by a wisdom greater than Wotan's to bring the "eternal feminine" into a world where the masculine mind alone would inevitably fail.

Wotan's will faltered when Fricka mercilessly destroyed his illusion. His dream of the emergence of a free man had been based on his hope to gain a friendly foe. Was not Siegmund the fruit of his love to a mortal woman, and foe only insofar as no longer dependent on the gods? Once grown strong and master of his own fate by virtue of heroic deeds and trials, he might no longer fully trust and blindly obey the gods; but his heart would forever belong to his father, and his rule, while free, would loyally serve Wotan's lofty aims.

Wotan no longer believes that a god can bestow freedom on a mortal. He now wants to remove from the earth all that has remained of his shattered hopes. But by abandoning his plan and seeking to destroy Sieglinde's unborn child, he frees that child forever from his rule. For a man born against the will of a god can never be his creature.

Wotan's farewell to Brunnhilde belongs musically and dramatically to the great achievements of human genius. Her plea for forgiveness stills the anger of the god, who senses in her parting words the will of one immeasurably greater than he. Like the Olympians of distant Greece, the devas of India, and the angelic hosts of the Hebrews, the Germanic gods were but fallible servants of the One. In all revelations of ancient mysteries there are stories of errant gods and fallen angels. In spite of all the resisting and deviating powers in heaven and on earth, the descent of the spirit to become flesh continued on its course, notwithstanding failures and sufferings, sacrifice and loss.

Wotan gave much of his own divine substance to men when he "fathered" Siegmund and Sieglinde. Now that Brunnhilde is to become mortal, he loses the heart of his heart. Pleading not to be left to the mercy of a man unworthy of her, the Valkyrie reminds Wotan that her soul is part of his own, and that the god himself would be dishonored in her. To one only can she belong: to him who is to be born against Wotan's will and thus blessed, or cursed, with the gift of freedom. But Wotan has learned his lesson; were he to lead Siegfried to Brunnhilde, he would interfere with destiny again and thus doom him to failure. One thing only can he do. He surrounds Brunnhilde's sleeping form with a ring of fire, impenetrable to all but him who knows no fear.

Chapter III

THE MYTHOLOGY IN WAGNER'S SIEFRIED

In the state of consciousness prevalent at the beginning of recorded history, man experienced himself as a mere tool of the gods. Good or evil fortune, health or sickness, even character traits: all lay "in the lap of the gods." Modern thinking is inclined to interpret ancient fatalism as an indication of superstition and ignorance. Yet the mere fact that virtually all the lofty ideas mankind now enjoys arose in ancient times ought to make modern scholars pause before judging too hastily what they do not understand.

Ancient man did not invent the gods; he experienced them in the mysteries of the starry heavens, in the miracle of life and death, in the elements and the seasons, in heredity, and in his own fate. During the course of evolution, basic changes occurred in his relationship to the immortals. When immediate intuitive perception faded it was gradually replaced by dogma and rituals that in turn were only too often misused by a power-hungry priesthood. As man's intuitive perception waned, however, the strength of his individuality waxed. In its descent to become flesh, the spirit, once at home with the immortals, came down to earth, strengthening man's self-awareness while the lights of Olympus and Valhalla dimmed.

With the changing relationship between gods and men, the longing to rule its own destiny was kindled in the human race. This longing, like every new impulse in the history of consciousness, found expression at first in the hearts and deeds of a few who outpaced their fellow men on the path of evolution. Such individuals became rebels against the power of the gods, and although their struggle often ended in personal tragedy, they were immortalized in songs and legends as the true heroes of their age. Jason, Hercules, Orion, and many others won their immortal victories not in wars against men, but on the battlefield of the spirit. In ancient Greece it was Prometheus, and from a different aspect, Oedipus, who represented man's fight against predestination. In German mythology it was Siegfried.

In Wagner's music drama, Wotan's plan for Siegmund and Sieglinde to be his heirs to rule the world failed. There was little the god could do then but attempt to destroy the new race of men. Too willful to submit to the older order, they were not as yet endowed with the true kind of freedom that gladly bows to superior wisdom. Wotan had ordered Brunnhilde to carry out his decision; but in defiance she had tried to save Siegmund, and when this failed, had led Sieglinde to a place where Wotan's power held no sway. It was the enchanted forest in which Fafner guarded the Ring and the hoard, and where Alberich and Mime lay in wait for them.

Alberich and Mime are brothers in darkness. Alberich represents evil in its transcendental form. He has renounced love forever, and thus has turned against God Himself and all His creatures. Mime represents evil on a lower level, that of ordinary existence, motivated by lust for power and by greed. His abode in the wild forest offers the only refuge for Sieglinde in the hour of her need; it is there she gives birth to Siegfried — and dies.

Mime, fully aware of the unique nature of the child, raises Siegfried as his own son. It is neither love nor pity that motivates him, but the hope that Siegfried will grow strong enough to slay the dragon and win for Mime the treasure of the Nibelungs, and with it the Ring of power over men and gods. The flaw in Mime's reckoning, however, is that Siegfried grows up to despise his foster father, whom he taunts and defies.

At last the day comes when Siegfried compels Mime to tell him the truth about his birth. Pressed for proof of the story, the dwarf brings forth the shards of the sword Sieglinde had carried as her only possession. It is Needful, Wotan's gift to Siegmund in his hour of greatest need, the gift that Wotan had later shattered by the still greater power of his sacred spear. Siegfried demands that Mime weld the pieces and restore the sword at once. Although a master in the ancient art of weapon forging, Mime has cast one sword after another for the boy, only to see each one shattered like a toy in Siegfried's strong hand. Mime gives in to despair; without Needful the youth cannot slay the dragon. But Mime instinctively feels that this sword of the gods can be mended only by the gods themselves, or by a mortal who does not fear them.

Roused from his despair, Mime is confronted by a stranger. It is Wotan who, disguised as a wanderer, restlessly roams the world. A joust takes place, a game of life and death, hardly comprehensible to modern thinking but an integral part of myths and legends from around the globe. It is the game of the sphinx, a game in which the contestants stake their lives. According to folk tradition, a challenge of such kind could not be declined. The contestant who is unable to answer one single question, of a kind regulated by tradition, forfeits his head. Mime, challenged, has the right to ask the first question. Secretive, suspicious, and in fear of revealing his plot to a stranger, he spurns the opportunity of asking for a solution to his own problem. Instead he asks and receives answers that have no practical value for him.

Now it is Wotan's turn. After two questions easily answered by Mime, the stranger asks the third: "Tell me, wise maker of weapons, who will, from the mighty shards, make the sword Needful whole again?" This is exactly the problem Mime has pondered in vain for years; and so, incapable of giving the right answer, he forfeits his life. While turning to leave, Wotan speaks the ominous words: "Guard well thy life — I give it, forfeited, to him who knows no fear."

The first act of Siegfried consists of three separate parts woven into one magnificent whole. The first of these parts offers a brief glimpse into Siegfried's upbringing from childhood to adolescence. The second part shows us the polite but deadly contest between the two adversaries, each of whom desperately seeks to use Siegfried for his own ends. The contest leads to a quick defeat of Mime, doomed to die at the hand of him who knows no fear. The third part deals with two psychological mysteries so complex that they can be discussed here only in the most sketchy manner. These mysteries are expressed in the inner experience of learning fear and forging the sword to control it. Mime, for reasons of his own, is anxious for Siegfried to have these experiences, but in reversed order. Only the fearless can mend Needful, the sword of the gods, which alone can slay Fafner and win the Ring for the dwarf; but because Mime's head is forfeited to the fearless, he can hope to escape doom only if the boy learns from Fafner the secret of fear. Siegfried fulfills the first task in his own reckless way: he files down and melts the pieces of the broken weapon, and from the fiery liquid casts a sword of his own.

One of the most ancient archetypes is the image of the sword. Countless other weapons have come and gone, but even today, in the age of missiles and nuclear fission, the image of the sword is still supreme. For the sword is more than a weapon against foes of flesh and blood. It symbolizes will power, the power which, if used correctly, can conquer the evil in our soul. Its slender, radiant blade is an image of the rays of the sun, bringing light into darkness. With its point turned downward, it has always been a symbol of peace, and it is more than chance that its hilt has the shape of the cross. In the ancient mysteries, the sword was not so much a symbol of destruction as the sign of victory through peace, victory over the forces of evil within and without. It is not mere coincidence that the name of Wagner's hero, Siegfried, means victory through peace. Thus, since time immemorial, St. Michael's sword appears in legends and myths as the image of creative will, its blade of light subduing the dragon on earth.

If man wants to be free and to subdue the dragon in himself, he must learn to wield a sacred sword. Therefore Wotan gave the sword of cosmic wisdom to his son Siegmund, to help him become the first free man. Yet it is not enough to accept passively the gift of power from the gods, for they can take back what they have given, and freedom that can be revoked is not freedom at all.

Unlike Siegmund's destiny, Siegfried's was not shaped by Wotan. His only heritage was a broken sword — of divine substance, but useless. Wagner hints here at one of the basic secrets of freedom: human will is a divine gift that becomes free only when recreated by man in the image of his own ideals. Siegfried had no difficulty in reforging the sword. Would Fafner teach him the secret of fear?

The second act gives the answer. Fafner, mightiest of the mighty, builder of Valhalla, owner of the Ring of power, giant turned monster, moves Siegfried to amusement and eventually anger, but not to fear.

Legends of old praised champions for their courage, and yet some of the most profound tales deal with a hero's longing for the experience of fear; for a man who has not had this experience is not courageous in the sense of later days. If he has been *created* fearless, he is deprived of one aspect of freedom. In olden times, when biological stamina played a much greater part in psychological responses than it does today, cowardice may indeed have been unknown to some legendary heroes. Siegfried was to remain a stranger to fear for the entire span of his life, and we shall see later that this eventually contributed to his doom.

As was the first act, the second is composed essentially of three parts. In the dark primeval forests in which no one but Fafner rules, Wotan and Alberich, the two great opponents of old, meet for the last time. Both have lost their power, and both have matured since their fatal encounter in the realm of the gods. Wotan no longer wants the Ring for himself; his only desire is to forestall the evil it would bring to the world in Alberich's hand. Alberich, too, has matured, but only in the intensity of his hate and the strength of his cunning. The confrontation between the two, though inconclusive, is an integral part of the message the Ring cycle conveys to modern man, regarding the profound change of consciousness that took place in the first millenium before Christ.

The ancient laws of virtue, which in spite of inadequacies had provided moral support for thousands of years, were rapidly losing ground. No longer did the gods have the power or even the desire to enforce their will. "Whom I love, I leave to his own designs. He stands or falls alone." And while traditional morality is on the wane, the compelling power of evil waxes. Will the Siegfried in man be strong enough to resist it?

In the central part of the second act, Siegfried kills Fafner and Mime. What interests us here is the once exalted, later terrifying, and finally pathetic figure of Fafner. The dragon has always been a favorite subject of myth and folklore. Scholarly interpreters have by and large taken one of two opposing views on the origin of the dragon legend. While one faction holds that the monster has a purely psychological and symbolic meaning, the other sees in it a lingering memory of the saurians of old. Neither interpretation is entirely satisfactory. The dragon, like so many mythological images, was once the object of immediate experience, familiar to those still endowed with intuitive vision. Originally the dragon was worshiped, especially among the Chinese; later, with the changing of consciousness, it became a symbol of decadent psychic forces. Residues of such forces are apt to linger in the unconscious mind, to become the mortal enemy of newer impulses, especially that of individuation.

Like every archetypal reality, the dragon took shape on two different planes of existence. It manifested itself in a natural phenomenon, in the saurians of ancient times, and it emerged as a symbol — a psychological one — representing no more, no less, than the faded memory of a once-powerful intuitive reality. Fafner was originally the representative of a human race endowed with dreamlike but immensely powerful magic faculties, the builder of forgotten cultures whose remains are even in our time an enigma and object of wonder. Misuse of spiritual power caused the downfall of many such cultures. Yet while great civilizations fell into oblivion, the misdirected spiritual longing that destroyed them remained in the subconscious minds of later generations, persisting throughout the centuries. This longing and the ever-recurring attempts to fulfill it by devious means are symbolized by the man-devouring dragon. Every individual has a dragon in his subconscious mind, which he must overcome lest he fall victim to the forces of darkness within. From senseless cruelty and unmotivated crime to the emergence of so-called progressive ideologies that in fact revive atavistic impulses, the forces of the dragon are even today on the rampage.

Siegfried, the proponent of a new phase of consciousness, has the strength to slay the dragon. He also kills Mime, who represents all that is faulty in the upbringing of a child. Wagner's libretto makes it clear that Siegfried kills the crude giant and the sly dwarf not out of malice but for reasons of inner necessity, thus transforming the forces he overcomes into faculties of a higher order. The young hero now becomes the owner of the Ring, of the divine power of selfhood, which, though tainted by the curse of Alberich, cannot harm him so long as his heart remains pure. The dragon blood torments the youth with burning fire; it represents the instinctive forces of animal nature welling up at the time of adolescence. But he who conquers them by the purity of his heart transforms the lower instincts of nature into an understanding of her higher aspects. Siegfried's sudden comprehension of the birds' language expresses the reward of such transformation in a most artistic and accurate way.

Just as the low instincts in man reflect all that is destructive in nature, all that threatens to pull him down to a subhuman level, sublimated desires respond to nature's intrinsic wisdom and magical beauty. In the brief time between adolescence and manhood, Siegfried lives an enchanted life. In the song of the birds he hears the call of his destiny, which, had he followed it to the end, would have taught him the secrets of love, happiness, and the meaning of life.

The threefold structure seen in the first and second acts can be discerned also in the third. The curtain rises on a scene of gloomy darkness rent by flashes of lightning. At the foot of a desolate mountain range, Wotan stands before the entrance to a cave. He summons Erda, the soul of the earth, from her sleep. Long ago she had ascended from her dark abode to seek the god in his sunlit domain. It was her warning that made Wotan yield the wrongfully acquired Ring to Fafner and Fasolt. When he, the proud ruler of gods and men, was faced with the superior wisdom intrinsic to the earth, he awoke to full recognition of his own responsibility in the curse against the Ring, and consequently to the knowledge that even a god may be tainted with guilt. He had discovered the existence of a master plan of creation that even the immortals could not defy with impunity.

To learn more of that master plan, he had followed Erda to her kingdom in the center of the earth, and from their union had sprung new evolutionary impulses personified in the nine Valkyries. But Wotan himself, in self-chosen exile, wandered on over the face of the earth, forever seeking the hero who might retrieve the Ring of power. Long since had he realized that no creature but man has the innate strength to defy Alberich, the prince of darkness. A man, but only one endowed with the supreme gift of freedom, could conquer the dragon, defeat Alberich, and save the world from doom. But Wotan also knew that not freedom, nor courage, nor innate strength could save the future master of the earth from failing, unless he learned to understand the wisdom of the past and became a pupil and friend of the gods whose heir he was to be.

"Siegfried" is the name given by later generations to a semi-legendary hero whose personality must have contained psychological stamina new to his era. He represented those who were the first to receive the fresh evolutionary impulses that were to be tried and tested in the crucible of life. Thus it is not surprising that one individual, or a small group, has time and again influenced the course of history and determined the fate of millions. Whenever experiments of such a kind are conducted for the sake of freedom, no one in heaven or on earth can predict their outcome. Since Siegfried is a representative of the Indo-Germanic races destined to play a major role in occidental culture, his attitude toward the past would decide between the chance for harmonious progress — and chaos. How would he use the Ring, the gift from the Creator of gods and men alike? Wotan seeks an answer to this question from the innate wisdom of the Earth; but in vain, for the price of man's freedom is the unpredictability of the use he will make of it. When Erda's vision fails, Wotan must face at last the irrevocable change that man's stewardship will bring to the world. Patiently he waits for the dawn of a new day, and for Siegfried, who unknowingly holds the key to the future.

The confrontation between Wotan and Siegfried, which constitutes the central part of the third act, throws light on a tragic flaw in human nature. Never seeming to learn that humility and self-imposed discipline, far from being incompatible with freedom are in reality its foundation, man tends to be either rebel or slave. Siegfried in particular reveals the potential greatness of the Germanic races, and their fateful limitations. He is the one man on earth of whom Wotan does not expect subservience, but neither is Wotan prepared for the degree of his arrogance. It had been the god's intent to hand over the reins of world dominion in peace, to reveal to Siegfried the tremendous power of the Ring now in his possession, the curse laid on it by Alberich, and the means of overcoming that curse. Yet Siegfried is a stranger not only to fear but also to reverence. The wise god means no more to him than the dragon he slew, and his impatience and touchiness are equally quick to be aroused. Angered by Wotan's smile, which he mistakes for condescension, and totally uninterested in the wisdom of the old, he orders the god to stand aside and let him pass.

If the sword is an ancient symbol of the forces of the sun (or of the moon, when curved like a scimitar), the spear with its long shaft points to a distance still farther beyond its wielder. In the hand of Wotan, the spear represents a stellar, cosmic power, fortified as it is by sacred runes. Although the god knows that his own strength cannot control the will of free man, he is still confident that the cosmic power entrusted to him can subdue it. Yet this time when the sword and spear clash, it is the god's weapon that breaks. In the framework of the legendary past, Siegfried's triumph over Wotan sets a precedent for the then-distant future, the time of man's supremacy on earth.

Centuries have gone by since the curtain rose on the era portrayed in *Rhinegold*. Then a state of consciousness had prevailed in which evolutionary impulses could not be envisioned but as deeds of the gods. In the era depicted in *Siegfried*, though the masses were still living and acting as in a dream world, some exceptional personalities had emerged who were already strongly motivated from a central focus within themselves. Such people were possessed of psychological faculties not yet shared by their fellow men, who in turn either looked up to them as leaders or persecuted them as destroyers of the old order. Whether such "heroes" were loved or hated, they were remembered in folklore as the trail-blazers of fate. Their lives, recorded not from a strictly historical point of view but from the far more realistic vantage point of inspired art, were seen as testing grounds for evolutionary impulses. The ordeals and deeds of a few exceptional persons would set the pattern for mankind as a whole; their victories could expand the scope of human consciousness, their failures diminish it.

In Wagner's work, at least where it reaches its summit, a strange phenomenon can be detected, the phenomenon of ancient wisdom being reborn in modern art. This unerring, instinctive wisdom reveals itself also in the fact that *Rhinegold* and *Valkyrie* still speak in the cold language of mythology, but *Siegfried* already emanates the magic warmth of the fairy tale. For the myth deals with destiny as made by the gods; the fairy tale with the inner life of man.

Siegfried's childhood reminds us of the childhood of many little princes and princesses in fairy tales. He too has an evil "stepfather," whose intent it is to use the child for his material ends and in the process to destroy his soul. Yet while the typical European fairy tale deals with the inner life of individuals belonging to a later era, an era on which Christianity has already left its imprint, Wagner's pagan hero is made of sterner stuff. In either case it is the power of heartless, greedy materialism that endangers the soul life of the child. As happens often in folklore, Siegfried finds refuge in the enchanted forest of childhood, in his communion with the wild creatures of nature.

Time passes, and childhood turns into adolescence with its tempest of roused instincts and fierce desires. It is interesting to observe here how much the attitude of the fairy tale and of great art differs from modern psychological teachings. Especially the Freudian school believes that biological desires must be satisfied rather than repressed, if man is to live in peace with himself and nature. The fairy tale knows better: springing from sources much closer to reality than intellectual conjecture, it is aware that nature's relationship with man differs basically from her relationship with the lower kingdoms. What modern psychologists forget is that desires are restricted in an animal by the safeguard of limited mating seasons and by many other controls totally absent in man.

In other words, man's very survival as a human being depends on his ability to control and sublimate nature by imposing on her his *spiritual* laws. This, of course, does not mean a return to "puritanism," which represents rejection rather than sublimation of nature, but an awareness of the fact that self-abandonment to animal desires will lead to the torment of addiction and mental unbalance rather than to fulfillment and emotional health. Just as the light and warmth-giving fire may turn into an all-devouring conflagration if permitted to burn uncontrolled, the sparks of uncontrolled desire tend to devour the core of man's being. Behind they will leave an empty shell. It is no coincidence that the dragon of old was depicted as a monster with fiery breath. His most tragic victims are the young, rendered defenseless by an upbringing that stresses all the wrong values of life. Just as the wolf, after devouring Red Riding Hood's grandmother, appears in the guise of his victim, so the dragon, replacing the very core of an adolescent's personality, may remain undetected by his environment. How surprised are parents and teachers when a "nice youngster" suddenly turns into a dope addict, a delinquent, or, hopelessly aware of his inner emptiness, throws away his life!

Siegfried resists Mime's wrong values, and, when the crucial moment comes, is strong enough to slay the dragon. Innocence in a child is a gift of the Creator, and ought to be jealously guarded by parents and teachers. Purity in an adolescent is the fruit of this first victory over the dragon; it opens the gates to true romanticism, which in turn is the secret of happiness, creativity, and the capacity for true love. Some of the world's greatest poets and painters have dedicated their lives to revealing the secrets of romanticism to the starving souls of modern men, but few have used means so artistically perfect as has Wagner.

When Siegfried swallows the drop of dragon blood that has spattered his finger, the world around him changes. The dark forest, which had housed the dragon and filled even the gods with terror, now is transformed into a place of enchantment. The twittering of a bird becomes a song whose message he can understand. It warns him of Mime's treachery and shows him the way toward love and happiness. Yet all this cannot fully convey the magic of romanticism, especially to a generation that has all but forgotten that youth can be happy. Here it is Wagner's music that speaks more clearly than words; it tells the secret of the life-span from adolescence to adulthood, which need not be tormenting but can be the most beautiful part of life.

Yet the years of youth are brief, and the sweet song

of Siegfried's winged friend gives way to the croaking of
Wotan's ravens. The young hero has passed many a test:
he has forged Needful without help from god or man,
slain the dragon, and calmed the burning fire of his senses.
Thus he has gained the rare happiness that opens to uncorrupted youth. Now a sterner test awaits him, the meeting with the god. This test, as we know, he fails; and
though the failure cannot prevent him from meeting
Brunnhilde, it leaves him poorly prepared to find through
her the real purpose of his life.

Brunnhilde's sleeping form is ringed by a wall of
fire that only the fearless can breach. Wagner refers here
obviously to a stage of the Mysteries of Initiation in which
the disciple had to brave a wall of fire to awaken his
"eternal bride." In *Siegfried* the absence of an officiating
priest is a major deviation from the traditional rule of
Initiation. This priest, or hierophant as the Greeks called
him, was to warn the novice of the terrific power of Initiation and its responsibilities and pitfalls. In Siegfried's
case, Wotan himself had assumed the part of the hierophant, but his help was rejected by the impatient youth.

Initiation into the Mysteries, during the age of paganism, was the prerequisite for all great leaders, and their
ordeals and experiences reached the general public only
in the guise of mythology and sacred art. The ordeals of
the novice were, of course, intuitive experiences that
must not be lightly dismissed as symbolic or unworldly.
Actually, the opposite is true, for a multitude of historical
records show that a person endowed with an innate or
carefully trained capacity for intuitive perception could
experience inwardly the causative factors leading to
outer events long before they were known to his fellow
men. Although the imagery of initiation experiences differs
slightly in the various mystery schools of the ancient

world, one image is common to all and has survived even the twilight of the pagan gods. In the fairy tale, it is the image of the "mystical wedding" of the prince who finds his princess; in *Siegfried*, of the hero who awakens his eternal bride. It signifies the union between man's conscious mind and the hidden powers of his soul. Formerly this union, if it took place in full consciousness, was considered the beginning of true humanity, since without it man knows neither himself nor the purpose of his life.

Quite apart from its cultic aspect, the concept of the mystical wedding refers also to any man's or woman's ability to recognize his rightful partner in life. A generation like ours, so addicted to psychology, especially to its views on the relationship of the sexes, could profit tremendously from a deeper understanding of sagas such as that of Siegfried and Brunnhilde.

The Valkyrie had found Siegfried in her heart before Wotan put her to sleep, and Siegfried had learned of Brunnhilde already when he, the dragon slayer, was roaming the enchanted forest in quest of high romance. Both Brunnhilde and Siegfried had passed the hidden tests that life itself puts to every child and youth; they had found in themselves the secret of the male and female principles. Because of it they were capable of supplementing each other as only separate human beings can do — separate and still interdependent, and thus able to find mutual happiness and real fulfillment in life. Their physical union, preceded as it had to be by the meeting of their souls, could find no appropriate expression except in the transcendent beauty of Wagner's music. And yet, although Siegfried has earned by his ordeals and inner victories the capacity for love and happiness, for meeting his eternal bride not only within but also as a woman of flesh and blood, he fails for the second time in a crucial test.

Wotan tried in vain to tell Siegfried of his origin and his mission, which could be fulfilled only with the help of the Valkyrie. Unprepared, Siegfried sees in Brunnhilde simply the woman he loves. She pleads with him to let their love mature before their bodies join, but Siegfried, who had unhesitatingly suppressed the dragon's fire in his own blood, sees no reason for restraining a passion sanctified by love. Had he listened to Wotan's warning or Brunnhilde's pleading, he would have understood that even true love needs a season of ripening, a period of pure romance, if it is to grow into perfection. For in man, love between the sexes has a purpose beyond that of procreation and the fulfillment of desires. It creates a mirror in which man can find himself and the purpose of his life. True to his proud and unyielding nature, Siegfried demands immediate fulfillment; and in the fire of passion, the mirror in which Siegfried should have seen his true image grows dim and cloudy.

Chapter IV

THE MYTHOLOGY IN WAGNER'S TWILIGHT OF THE GODS

The opera *Siegfried* relates the story of the world's greatest hero up to the time of his manhood. It brings to life the enchanted childhood and romantic youth of the legendary representative of the first free man. Stronger than the gods, stronger than destiny, invulnerable even to Alberich's curse, he can hold no one but himself responsible for the victory or defeat that will henceforth befall him. At his side Siegfried carries the sword he himself has forged: Needful, the invincible weapon. He has slain the dragon in his soul, and by this deed attained a gift of understanding the world that is beyond the grasp of other mortals. His union with Brunnhilde, his eternal bride, has endowed him with an inner strength and security that only love of the highest order can bestow on a man. With this union, the music drama *Siegfried* reaches its triumphant finale.

The Twilight of the Gods tells us the story of Siegfried's manhood: the radiantly hopeful beginning, the pitfalls, and the tragic end. To Wagner, Siegfried is far more than an individual; he represents the highest perfection man can achieve through his own efforts. But in him, mankind has been measured, weighed, and found wanting.

The curtain rises on a scene that reveals the end of an era in which the destiny of man was controlled by the gods and recorded in the weaving of the Norns, or Fates. It is a scene indicating Wagner's transcendental concept of the hero's fate, as expressed by the words and actions of the Norns. This mystical introduction is followed by Siegfried's farewell to Brunnhilde.

The all-important change in consciousness that takes place in the transition period between the romantic idealism of uncorrupted youth and the down-to-earth reality of manhood is so difficult to define that it is beyond the reach even of poetry. The only medium ideally suited to its expression is the greatest of all arts, music. Wagner, whose genius as composer surpasses even his gift for dramatic art, tells the story of this change in consciousness in the rhythms and harmonies of Siegfried's Rhine Journey.

The magnificent tone poem describes the jubilant mood of a youth who, after having won victory after victory in the crucial struggles of adolescence, has now set out to conquer the world. The triumphant Siegfried motif, a musical apotheosis of purity and joy — a challenge to battle, yet without a trace of hate or malice — rises upward, as it were, from the flowing waters of the mighty river Rhine. And from deeper levels the motif of the Rhine Maidens sings of their hope that Siegfried will renew the vital forces of the earth by restoring to the Maidens the stolen treasure of the sacred gold.

Siegfried's river journey, however, is not merely a joyous voyage up the vast expanse of the lower Rhine. It pictures a vital part of man's journey through life. In the latter part of the tone poem, a more serious strain of music mingles with the light-filled motifs of Siegfried, the Rhine and the Rhine Maidens. It is joyous, too, but of a distinctly different character, expressing the welcome of the world for a hero whose victories might be victories of peace rather than war, as his name implies. Yet the closer the youth comes to the end of his journey, the more clearly another, darker motif emerges, a motif conveying treachery and hate. The first station on Siegfried's journey is the hall of the Gibichungs. Here he will have to meet his first test as a man. The scene that follows, transcends, as in all of Richard Wagner's dramas, the merely personal fate of the hero.

A small group of people is expecting the arrival of Siegfried. Each of them is a person in his or her own right as well as a prototype deeply rooted in the historical setting of the era. King Gunther, the lord of the castle, and his younger sister, Gutrune, are representatives of average man, though of the most refined and respected stratum of civilization. Gunther must be envisioned as a just and brave lord, beloved by his people, earnestly striving to uphold the strict moral standards of Germanic tribes; his sister, as a paragon of maidenly virtue and devotion to her brother. This small family group, whose moral strength is rooted solely in tradition and upbringing, is no match for the sinister influence of Hagen, their half-brother and the son of the dwarf, Alberich.

Hagen is the ever-present but seldom recognized representative of evil, to whose superior knowledge and cunning the ignorant realist falls victim only too easily. With the emergence of freedom in human consciousness, as expressed in Siegfried's victory over the gods, super- and sub-human beings had lost their compelling power over man's destiny. The battle for the human soul was no longer fought in Valhalla or in Alberich's dark realm, but in the psyche of man. Alberich, aware of the changing conditions of destiny, had sired Hagen, a mortal, to achieve what he could no longer accomplish by himself: regain the Ring and by its power enslave the world.

In ancient times, the secrets of man's true nature, and of the forces that determine his fate, were contemplated in the great temple universities of paganism all over the civilized world. Though men were fully aware of the important role that heredity plays in the shaping of the physiological and psychological organism of a human being, they did not think that the innermost core of the human being was the product of purely biological forces. This innermost core, called by the Greeks the entelechy or daemon of man, was credited with qualities unique to the individual, apart from the characteristics of the body he inhabited. The concept of entelechy corresponded roughly with the Judeo-Christian concept of an immortal soul.

Most pagan creeds held that the human entelechy neither begins nor ends with life on earth. Man's "mortality" referred merely to the fact that his self-awareness ceased with the death of his body. The immortal gods differed from mortal man by the continuation of their consciousness. Since ancient ideas on the mystery of birth cannot be separated from pagan philosophies about the soul's supersensible existence, certain conceptions generally accepted in the pre-Christian era should be mentioned.

According to pagan theology, consciousness after death could reach one of three different levels. The first level was the one allotted to the average man: dreamlike, with almost complete absence of memory and self-identification, called Hades in Greek, Hel in German mythology. The second was accessible to the true hero, the man whose deeds of courage and creativeness distinguished him from ordinary mortals. The Greeks called this state of consciousness the Elysian Fields, the Germans, Valhalla. The third level was reached by those who could soar beyond the narrow limits of earth-bound consciousness, and thus bring new impulses into the world. Already while they still lived in a mortal body, their awareness had assumed divine status. Their souls after death, in the language of mythology, were lifted to the stars.

Although the influence of biological heredity on the physiological and emotional characteristics of the child were well-known, the spiritual attitude of a woman during the moment of conception was considered to be of even greater importance. While her physical union determined the biological organism of the offspring, her spiritual union determined the kind of entelechy that would inhabit this organism. If she loved her partner not only with her body but also with her soul, the offspring would be the true child of his mortal father. This, however, was not always desired. To bring into the world a being greater than his sire, a woman would under some circumstances consummate her marriage in a trance-like state of consciousness, at times within the precincts of a temple, so that a god might be the true "father" of her child.

Whether or not such ideas are acceptable to our thinking, they are indispensable for an understanding of ancient culture and thought life. One of the many examples that could be cited is that of Alexander the Great. Although fully recognized as Philip's son, he was, long before the time of his fame, accepted as a child of Apollo. And it is generally conceded today that he owed his successes at least partly to the conquered peoples' acceptance of his divine origin.

Concepts of good and evil in pagan theology differed vastly from Judeo-Christian ideas. Gods of war and destruction were worshipped and respected no less than gods of justice and healing. Temples and sanctuaries were dedicated to Moloch and Ares and other gods of darkness who promised their followers wealth, power, and fulfillment of carnal desires. In Wagner's *Ring*, Alberich represents such a spirit of darkness, and Grimhilde, Hagen's mother, must be seen as one of his worshippers. Her own hate and greed subjected her soul to Alberich's dark, vengeful spirit. Possessing no human body, he could nevertheless sire a son, Hagen, destined to challenge Siegfried and his mission on earth.

Siegfried, too, is of divine lineage, for both his father Siegmund and his mother Sieglinde were Wotan's children. Expressed differently, his personality contains some of the light, clarity, and elemental strength sensed at times in the mountain bastions of northern lands. These qualities he inherited from his parents, themselves conceived in a sanctuary of Wotan. To this heritage Siegfried added what no man before him had achieved, the self-forged sword of the free, self-reliant will.

Never could Hagen have conquered Siegfried in open combat, yet he owns a weapon that in the end brings him victory. This weapon is the dark wisdom of his father, Alberich, to which he obediently listens. Siegfried, reveling in the pride of independence, rejects the counsel of the gods of light. Thus the hero, while courageous, strong, and free, fails for lack of the wisdom that only humility can give to men.

What Siegfried lacks is still alive in Brunnhilde, for the Valkyrie, though reborn in a mortal body, has retained a trace of divine wisdom. Since Wagner's dramas, like other manifestations of truly great art, take place on different levels of reality, Brunnhilde represents not only a human being in her own right but also the feminine, the intuitive, part of Siegfried's psyche. And Hagen knows that Siegfried can be conquered only when separated from his eternal bride and deprived of the echo of her wisdom in his own heart.

Like all born leaders — and "misleaders" — of men, Hagen is a discerning judge of human character. He knows how to persuade Gunther and Gutrune to offer a love potion to Siegfried, skillfully lulling their feeble, traditional conscience to sleep. In contrast to the happy endings of contrived stories, the invincible hero falls an easy victim to the clumsy device. Unsuspecting, he accepts the potion whose power attracts him irresistibly to Gutrune while it extinguishes his memory of Brunnhilde, his eternal bride.

Critics of Wagner the dramatist have pointed out that the hero's defeat by such an unimaginative and apparently unavoidable trap invalidates the artistic significance of the whole drama. These critics fail to realize that Wagner uses the symbols best suited to express the tests invariably demanded by fate of its chosen. For the true hero is set apart precisely by his ability to comprehend and accomplish what is beyond the reach of average men. Many of the tests and ordeals described in religious tradition, mythology, and fairy tales demand the impossible. In Siegfried's case, Wagner has left no doubt that what indeed might have been impossible for lesser men was well within the scope of his hero's gifts.

The youth's intuitive perception, essential to the true

leader, is one of the main themes of the opera *Siegfried*. Victory over the dragon, and ability to transform its blood, enable the hero to understand the language of nature. Even the elusive birds of the forest are no longer insignificant little creatures, but in their twitterings reveal to his enlightened soul a message of supernal wisdom. This gift of discovering truth beyond the facade of mere appearance has given Siegfried also the power to discern behind Mime's friendly words the voice of treachery and hate. Mime, too, had offered Siegfried a poisoned draught that would have ended his mission, had his heart not been pure enough to perceive the truth. The tragic guilt that makes Siegfried the unsuspecting victim of Hagen's deceit lies in the almost imperceptible deterioration of his innermost being. The hero who fights for the good of the world must always expect hate and treachery. To attain his quest, he must in humility keep awake the voice of his heart, which alone can warn him in moments of peril.

One of the gifts of the creative artist is his ability to convey messages on various levels simultaneously, without sacrificing artistic truth on any of them. Siegfried's falling victim to Hagen's plot serves as an example. Wagner's scripts make it eminently clear that love potions in his dramas do not mean simply an adulterous draught, but denote assault on an entirely different level than the physical one. Nevertheless, even were we to take at face value Siegfried's acceptance of the love potion, we could not consider him the innocent victim of an unavoidable trap. For the very prerequisite for a mission on earth is the hero's ability to see beyond the surface appearance of his environment. Thus the use of a seemingly obvious plot enables Wagner to call our attention to the true reason for Siegfried's failure, which lies in the coarsening of his intuitive perceptiveness. So crucially important is this fact that, at the risk of his own life, Hagen, Siegfried's mortal enemy, contemptuously alludes to it before striking the fatal blow.

The further course of the drama implies that the potion that makes Siegfried forget both Brunnhilde and his mission is also symbolic of a weakness excusable perhaps in average men but potentially fatal to the true hero. This weakness may in modern terms be called infatuation of a sensual origin.

Siegfried has been exposed to three fundamental trials that concern any human being's attitude toward love and sex. The first test is a man's confrontation with the dragon, a contest in which the dragon represents sex as an end in itself. An individual unwilling or unable to control this monster is eventually dehumanized by its insatiable demands.

Unfortunately, a rather vociferous group among modern psychologists still advocates sexual permissiveness. This attitude stems from the illusory hope that the abandonment of erotic inhibitions will lead to sexual satisfaction and contentment. Actually, desires can be satisfied only within the scope of their natural or spiritual aims. Indulgence in appetites that serve neither must lead inevitably to the danger of addiction, with its disastrous effects on a person's emotional and physical health.

What are the natural and spiritual aims of sexual desire? In animals, they fulfill a clearly defined biological function, namely procreation, and therefore preservation of the species. Thus sexual desire in the animal kingdom is entirely extroverted. Man's biological organism, being animal-like too, must suffer if his libido is not directed toward the opposite sex. But in man, and in man alone, desires are also expressions of spiritual longings, which permit him to modify and even overrule his biological nature. His attitude toward sex, which as the physical manifestation of love, represents the most powerful of his urges, will crucially determine his fate. Just because man's mind differs radically from the instinct of animals, owing to the fact that he is not compelled by instinct to follow biological laws, he may be attracted to a partner who does not ideally fulfill his purely physical needs. But whether man's sexual desire follows spiritual laws, or biological, or both, it must radiate and never, never turn back on himself. Since the common principle of biological as well as spiritual love is its tendency to offer itself up, the degree of physical satisfaction depends largely on a person's ability to give rather than to receive.

Whenever desire ceases to serve either a spiritual or a biological goal, and seeks nothing but its own fulfillment, a personality split occurs. For the mind of an individual remains integrated only so long as his emotions and actions remain subject to the unifying control of reason. Undoubtedly there is always some sort of reason in seeking pleasure, but whenever the fulfillment of biological desires becomes an end in itself, pleasure soon becomes the victim of glandular and neurological exhaustion. Cravings indulged with diminishing chance for fulfillment lead to the torment of addiction. In other words, a part of the psyche hostile to man's physical and emotional well-being assumes control and eventually devours his rational selfhood. That this legendary dragon, monster, hydra, or whatever else it may be called is not limited to the area of sex, is self-evident. In the compulsive eater, alcoholic, drug addict and sexually obsessed, one common condition holds sway: defeat by the dragon.

Siegfried has passed this first test, and by doing so has avoided the soul-destroying power of narcissism. His victory has made him capable of love and of finding the woman who, though an individual in her own right, supplements the best part of his own psyche. In the intuitive language of art, he has found his soul mate, his eternal bride. The second trial, however, tested his willingness to transform his own being by the power of his love for a woman, before demanding physical consummation.

The union between Siegfried and Brunnhilde is, musically at least, mankind's greatest artistic expression of true love. It was not the physical consummation in itself that caused failure, but Siegfried's unwillingness to curb his impatience for the sake of chivalry. Had he possessed this possibly greatest of all manly qualities, chivalry, he would have listened to Brunnhilde's pleas and postponed physical union until such time as his feeling for Brunnhilde had pervaded his whole being. Short of such a transformation, he approached his third trial unprepared.

In this third test, the ultimate struggle for the dominance of the soul over the body or of the body over the soul, Siegfried fails. In the turmoil of his aroused senses, his memory of Brunnhilde wanes and, forgetting her, he becomes a mere mortal. A man who has betrayed the sacred pledges of his past cannot fulfill the promises of his future. Once "the world's greatest hero," Siegfried no longer differs from those he had been destined to save. Hagen plots his death, but his fate on earth is no longer of great consequence.

Siegfried, the hero, is dead. Siegfried, the man, walks blindly into the trap set by Hagen. To win Gutrune for his wife, he returns once more to the enchanted world of his youth and his first, now forgotten, love. The ring of fire that protects Brunnhilde from all but the bravest of men can be passed by Siegfried alone. Yet he does so in the guise of Gunther, who has promised him his sister if Siegfried can win Brunnhilde for him.

Siegfried's betrayal of Brunnhilde does not spring from intentional disloyalty, but from spiritual amnesia. Yet while he is no longer aware of the bond that ties his soul to the soul of Brunnhilde, he still remembers the golden ring on her finger, which he had once given her as pledge of everlasting faith. It is the cursed Ring of the Nibelung, fashioned by Alberich from the sacred treasure of the Rhine. When Siegfried takes the Ring back, he does not know of its tremendous power, nor of the curse that Alberich has put on it. Only the pure are immune to this curse; Siegfried, no longer pure, is subject to its deadly threat.

The scenes that follow depict the double wedding of Gunther to Brunnhilde and Siegfried to Gutrune; they also bring to the stage one of the most dramatic events of the tetralogy. Brunnhilde's accusation of Siegfried, his solemn oath of innocence, and Hagen's murderous plot are well-known to all admirers of Wagner's dramatic art. Less attention has been given to the almost unfathomable depth to which Wagner probes the mysteries of "tragic guilt," the failure before God, which may occur even though no human law be broken.

Wagner rediscovers here the long-lost key to a deeper understanding of evil. Evil in its darkest form does not depend on wicked deeds, nor even on bad intentions. For actions and aims can be corrected, atoned for, or at least repented. But when man permits his awareness to grow dim, when he takes a step backward on his path of moral evolution, he commits a sin against the meaning of existence, the sin against the Holy Ghost. Such failures bring suffering to the world, suffering far greater than any caused by intentional evil.

The paradox of the innocently guilty, so incomprehensible to the merely intellectual thinking of our time, was once a wellspring of artistic inspiration. Highly intuitive people, especially the Greeks, still understood the tragic guilt of an Oedipus and Orestes. In our time, no words can express what only the heart can understand. But the language comprehensible to the heart is music. And Wagner used this language to express the otherwise inexpressible. In the music that accompanies Siegfried's oath of innocence in the face of Brunnhilde's accusation, Wagner lifts for a moment the veil from the hidden mystery of evil. In its ultimate sense, evil is the dimming of consciousness, the sullying of the mirror that in the course of evolution is destined to reflect the godhead in man. Is it coincidence that Siegfried's fall is symbolized as the effect of a mind-changing — mind-darkening — drug?

The third act of the music drama consists of three distinctly different parts. The first, ending with Siegfried's death at the hand of Hagen, shows again Wagner's intuitive grasp of psychology and his unfailing insight into the real causes of human failure. On a hunting expedition arranged by Hagen and Gunther, Siegfried has momentarily strayed from his companions. Pursuing a bear to the bank of the Rhine, he suddenly finds himself in the presence of three beautiful maidens. They are the Rhine Maidens, who seek to persuade Siegfried to give back to them the Ring fashioned from the gold of the Rhine. In a mood of bitter humor, Wagner brings into focus the tragic character changes that have reduced Siegfried to a mere mortal. He who in his youth knew so well how to see spiritual reality behind natural phenomena, is now totally incapable of distinguishing between intuitive vision and sensual perception. He is quite willing to yield the Ring, whose power he does not crave, in exchange for an amorous adventure.

The love potion given to Siegfried by Gutrune, the intoxicating poison of soulless passion, has made him forget and betray his eternal bride. It does not prevent him from seeking adventure, an adventure that would lead to breaking faith with his young wife, Gutrune, whom he has won at such a high price. Once generous to a fault, he now rejects the plea of the Rhine Maidens to give them the Ring, which he hardly values, without exacting from them the promise of a fleeting moment of lust. The Rhine Maidens' warning of impending disaster has no effect on him, for his courage is still unshaken. But while it was once the courage of the true hero, it has now deteriorated to mere boldness, the boldness of a man not mature enough to have learned the meaning of fear.

When Siegfried rejoins the hunting party, his last chance for survival has passed. As so often in real life, the man marked by death remembers the long-forgotten dreams of his youth. Prodded by Hagen, he tells his companions the true story of his life, haltingly at first, then more and more fluently. As he does so, his inner sight begins to return. What in the beginning of his tale he describes as the "prattle" of a bird becomes again the voice of man's truest friend, the voice of unspoiled nature. In the song of a bird, in the cawing of a raven, Siegfried is reminded of the wisdom that once guided him in his quest. And when at last he remembers Brunnhilde, the soul of his soul, he has found himself again and reawakens to his mission. Too late; for this is the moment when Hagen thrusts his spear into Siegfried's heart.

The second part of the last act reveals its dramatic message by the music alone. According to Wagner's stage directions, Siegfried's body is carried on his shield in almost total darkness, until at last the silvery light of the moon breaks through the cover of clouds. The drama now finds its sole expression in the magnificent music of the Funeral March, which is reminiscent of Siegfried's Rhine Journey, though it moves, as it were, in the opposite direction. While the latter begins with triumphant joy and hope, descending to a mood of foreboding and sadness, the former follows the road back from grief to hope.

In its early part, the music of the Funeral March tells a story of grief surpassing the sorrow over even a great hero's death. It expresses stark tragedy, as if the mute hope of all creatures, as so often in man's tragic history, has been shattered again, and for the final time. The symphony of despair over man's plight, and of fierce rebellion against fate, appears to rise upward in a futile accusation of the immortal gods. But it is not futile; for after a brief moment of hopeless resignation, the wrath of earth's creatures finds its mark in the heights. Intermingled with the majestic motif of the immortals, the music raises the mood of doom to a higher level, ringing the death knell of the pagan era, the twilight of the gods. As if the world were holding its breath, a strange mood of calm prevails for a short while, until, hesitating at first and then more and more triumphant, the motif of Siegfried comforts the grieving world with a message of hope. As if on a canvas woven of sounds, Wagner paints once more the panorama of Siegfried's life. He retraces its course, compassionately disentangling the threads where their pattern went wrong, until the radiant image of his youth, his love for Brunnhilde, and his mission emerge unsullied and timeless.

Siegfried's Funeral March, in all its tragedy, is also a testimony to the triumph of man's eternal hope for ultimate salvation. Men, even the greatest, may fail; but ideals, once conceived, can eventually prevail. In the final strains of the musical interlude, Brunnhilde's leitmotif mingles with that of Siegfried. Siegfried the man is dead, but his spirit lives again and will once more be united with hers. The hero's mission has failed, but Brunnhilde, through the sacrifice of her life, will prevent the Ring from falling into Hagen's hands and thus save the world from the rule of evil.

In the third part of its final act, the tetralogy of the *Ring* operas rises above the level of human striving and error. It takes on a mystical and universal aspect that can be discussed only in conjunction with the transcendental opening scene of the *Twilight of the Gods.*

We know that legends and myths are almost always woven around historical personalities. Why have such people attained the immortality of heroes? Rarely by virtue of outer achievement, but because they represented, or rather introduced at deadly peril, a new impulse in human consciousness. A minor war lord like King Arthur attained immortality not by virtue of his transitory victory over the Saxons, but because he was credited with the concept of the Round Table and the quest of the Holy Grail. Even today, few Englishmen will scoff at the legend prophesying that their country's spiritual greatness will be restored when King Arthur returns to earth. And why is it that in German folklore Friedrich Barbarossa is still alive beneath the Kyffhauser mountain, waiting for the hour to make his country pure and great again? Historically, the rule of Friedrich I was tragic rather than successful. But instinctively the people felt the greatness of his concept of their country's peaceful mission on earth.

Most heroes left no historical imprint of their deeds. In Wagner's conception, Siegfried was such a hero. Understanding his figure could shed light on the meaning of history, provided his story is envisioned as a chapter within the book of mankind itself. Thus *The Twilight of the Gods* begins and ends with events that appear to dwarf all human deeds. And yet they are indispensable for the comprehension of Siegfried's mission, for they show a master plan for evolution, which man's will is free to further or to thwart.

As mentioned at the beginning of this chapter, the First Act curtain rises on a mysterious scene. The distant fire ringing the rock of the Valkyries throws a flickering light on three unearthly figures: the Norns, weavers of the pattern of destiny. These mythological figures have existed in the lore of almost all ancient peoples. They were also known as Fates, Parcae, and Moirai. They have always represented servants of the highest God, weaving and recording the deeds of His creatures into an inescapable web of cause and effect. Their power ends when one day a hero arises, the first man fearless enough to accept the greatest gift the Creator has to offer, the gift of free choice.

This fateful day in evolution is the real subject of Wagner's tetralogy, and it is certainly no coincidence that its final work opens with the last chapter of the Norns' power on earth. For the last time they recall the past, conjuring up some chapters from the book of evolving consciousness. The first Norn sings of the World Ash, to whose trunk, eons ago, had been fastened the golden cord of destiny. This was the time when the earth was young and before individual consciousness had come fully into existence. The legendary tree, also known as the tree of life, symbolized the vital forces of growth that ruled supreme in the childhood age of the earth. Then the planet was teeming with life, a gigantic breeding place of unlimited vitality. Species abounded, mutated, and gave way to better-equipped forms of life. Destiny seemed to seek only one goal: biological evolution. This was the golden age of the Norns.

Eventually, however, self-awareness sprang up on earth, disrupting the cosmic order of cause and effect by the first stirrings of self-seeking will. Wotan was the first representative of this impulse, according to the mythology of Germanic cultures, just as Lucifer and Prometheus had been according to other creeds. In recalling the past, the Norns tell of the god who once drank deeply from the wellspring of wisdom, and paying for it with the loss of one eye, cut the shaft of his spear from the trunk of the World Ash. The spear gave Wotan power over the earth by virtue of rules and agreements he had made with its inhabitants. They were the first laws, strictly adhered to in ancient pagan theocracy. The World Ash, however, never recovered from its wound. In time it withered and died.

What is the hidden meaning of this ancient story? It signifies the appearance of consciousness, of self-awareness apart from the all-encompassing wisdom of primordial creation. Consciousness, however, stands in opposition to life, as shown by the limited powers of growth and regeneration that characterize conscious beings as compared with the far greater vitality manifest in lower species. Wotan's mutilation of the World Ash is a deeply meaningful image, revealing in artistic language a basic secret of evolution. It refers to the once creative impulse from which all higher forms of evolving consciousness spring. Just as a river must lose some of its elemental power if that power is to be transformed into a more sophisticated form of energy, primeval earth's gigantic life forces had to dwindle if higher forms of consciousness were to appear.

The god's deed was also the first step toward the emergence of freedom, for which he had sacrificed one of his eyes. Only a being willing to sacrifice a part of his inner sight could separate himself from his Creator in such a way as to lay the foundation for willful and possibly unwise action. With the emergence of individual consciousness a dam was created, stemming the free flow of biological evolution. The tree of the world started to wither, and the boundless vitality of primeval earth slackened. The golden cord of destiny was no longer fastened to the World Ash, but had to be transferred to another principle, expressed in the image of the hemlock.

In Indo-Germanic mythology, the hemlock was dedicated to the Saturnian Mysteries, the mysteries of self-awareness and death. When Wotan's power flourished by virtue of laws and agreements inscribed on the shaft of his sacred spear, the hemlock, according to the story of the second Norn, replaced the ash. It was the golden era of paganism, when whole tribes felt bound by sacred agreements to which their leaders had sworn in the temples of the gods. But this phase of evolution also passed. Individual thought life replaced tribal ethics, and the cord of destiny became fastened to "solid rock." Translated into less imaginative language, *individual* self-awareness and destiny, as determined by man's crystallizing intellect, began to emerge from the hard, mineral substance of the human skull.

With Siegfried, a new impulse came into the world. "Of divine origin," he was capable of freeing human will from the narrow scope of merely selfish aims. When his sword shattered Wotan's spear, the gods' power over human destiny came completely to an end, and the rule of the world was left to man. In the hands of the Norns, the golden cord broke. For neither gods nor Fates could then predict how man would make use of his freedom.

Siegfried failed in his mission to lead humanity into

a brighter, man-created future. Thus the cycle of the Ring would have ended in despair had the curtain fallen on the scene of Siegfried's inglorious death. But in her farewell to the world, Brunnhilde opens vistas of a new impulse that, after long sorrow and strife, may yet bring salvation to mankind.

> "May the gods perish with all their glory;
> May leaderless the world remain,
> Deprived of custom and law . . . .
> The power of love alone
> Can bring salvation in joy and woe."

The pagan priest sought to appease the gods by offering up the lives of other creatures, even those of human beings. Brunnhilde, in her final deed of love, offers *herself*, and in her sacrificial death restores the Ring to its true owners. There in its watery bed, it will rest until a new impulse can enter the world of man. This new era, for which Wagner longed from the depth of his troubled heart, finds its immortal expression in the crowning work of his life, *Parsifal*.

Chapter V

THE MYTHOLOGY IN WAGNER'S PARSIFAL

Richard Wagner's final work, his music drama *Parsifal*, was completed in 1882, just a year before the composer's death. Although different in content and message, *Parsifal* reminds one of Goethe's *Faust*. Each of these masterworks represents a declaration of faith by the world's greatest men. Both Goethe and Wagner, while remaining rather aloof from organized religion, dedicated their lives to the never-ending search for the spiritual meaning of existence. Signposts left behind them on their quest were magnificent works of art, reaching unparalleled perfection in *Faust* and *Parsifal*.

However, as in the case of *The Ring* tetralogy that preceded it, *Parsifal* could not exert its healing influence on an age so desperately in need of healing. Then as now, in spite of Wagner's pleas, his librettos were regarded as rather tiresome efforts on the part of a great composer to prove his dramatic skill, efforts condescendingly tolerated for the sake of his magnificent music. But the music, great as it is, represents merely the means by which the composer hoped to open the hearts of the audience to an understanding of the message of his dramas.

The story of Parsifal deals with one aspect of the legend of the Holy Grail, a legend deeply significant for the history of consciousness in the Christian era. Like the earlier paganism, Christianity has its Mysteries, of which its rites and rituals are but symbols. As in all great creeds, such symbols, originally understood to be clues to immediate intuitive experience, eventually became ends in themselves. In the golden age of paganism, the original wisdom of true religion lived on in the great temple schools of Thebes, Ephesus, Eleusis, and many other centers, giving birth to the lofty ideas of freedom, democracy, justice, and conscience. Christianity's esoteric core has lived on for more than a millennium in the Mystery of the Holy Grail.

According to some versions of the legend, the Grail is the vessel from which Jesus drank at the Last Supper, and in which Joseph of Arimathea gathered some of the blood that flowed from His wounds. Later the chalice was said to have been taken to England, where it was secretly worshiped until its disappearance in the fifth century. According to Rudolf Steiner, the Austrian scholar and philosopher, the worshipers of the Grail encountered in England yet another religious brotherhood, which, though Christianized, had its origin in druidic Mysteries. The most prominent leader of this brotherhood and the deeds of its gallant knights were later immortalized by Sir Thomas Malory in his *Morte d'Arthur*. During the first Christian centuries, the Church, not yet having assumed rigid control, permitted secret and semi-secret brotherhoods to carry out special cultural and spiritual tasks. Such groups were chiefly composed of members of the most highly respected estates of the era: the hermit-priests and the knights.

Malory, creating a vivid picture of such a brotherhood, describes how hermits, leading lives of complete religious dedication, served as advisers, confessors, and physicians to knights whose task it was to preserve a semblance of law and order in a chaotic age. With the breakdown of Roman justice, England and vast parts of continental Europe would have been entirely at the mercy of minor warlords who respected no law but their own, had there been no champions of God's justice. There is little doubt today that a group of highly respected knights did exist, traveling alone or in small groups from castle to castle, from village to village, to hear the complaints of the wronged and to take up their case against their oppressors. In such esteem were these champions held that their deeds have lived on ever since in legends and songs.

The earlier knighthood of the Grail seems to have pursued tasks somewhat different from those of the Arthurian brotherhood, which was also known as the Knights of the Round Table. At least during the first five centuries after Christ, its main objective was the preservation of the esoteric roots of Christianity. The relics most sacred to the knights of the Grail were the chalice and the spear, not only for their sacramental but also for their symbolic significance. Thus, according to the imagery used by Chrétien de Troyes and other medieval writers, the sacred cup symbolized the archetype of the human head, as transformed by thoughts of pure love. The spear represented creative forces reaching the earth from the universe. At one time held in undisputed possession by the gods, Wotan's spear, its shaft split asunder by Siegfried, fell into the power of mortals when at last they began to understand and to control natural laws.

In human hands, the once sacred spear became a symbol of power until the event of Golgotha, when the blade of a spear pierced the side of Jesus. Since, according to the mysticism of early Christianity, Jesus' blood, the *Sang Real*, contained divine properties, the weapon that shed this blood played a profound part in the transcendental drama of redemption. Consequently, the symbol of the spear, once the sacred weapon of Wotan, later a symbol of destruction, received a new significance. The hope arose that the gift for which it stood, man's growing power over nature, might eventually be transformed and used again for the good of mankind.

The exact location of the center of the Grail cult remained a well-kept secret, but outposts appeared all over Europe, from the coast of Spain to the shores of the Baltic Sea.

The mission of the order of the Grail, however, was not exclusively mystical. Combining the carefully trained gift of intuitive insight with political wisdom and selfless devotion, emissaries of the Grail seem to have served as advisers to statesmen, as educators, and even as generals when the very life-stream of occidental culture was in danger of extinction. Such emissaries, known to the folklore of almost all European nations, were bound by sacred vows to remain unrecognized until, their mission completed, they could return to the anonymity of the order.

Yet even the servants of the Grail, being human, were corruptible. According to many stories collected by Malory, their very leaders became decadent, and threatened to betray their sacred trust. This was the time when King Arthur's brotherhood, the afore-mentioned knighthood of the Round Table, found itself called upon to remove the Grail from the power of those knights no longer worthy

to be its guardians. This fact is indicated by the story of
Sir Galahad's being imprisoned for a year by a corrupt
king of the Grail.

It is interesting to note that some of the most serious
students of the Grail legend have asked: What was actually accomplished by the Arthurian quest of the Grail;
and why, if successful, was it followed by the darkest
centuries in occidental history? This question is clearly
answered by Malory. Galahad, after liberating the Grail
from guardians no longer worthy of its service, did not
bring the chalice back into the world, but removed it to
a sphere beyond the reach of human error and greed.

According to the tradition preserved in various parts
of Europe, the influence of the order of the Grail under-
went cyclic changes. Whenever Christian civilization
reached an impasse that might have marked its destruction, the Grail reappeared in the world, provided there
could be found on earth at least a few individuals dedicated and pure enough to serve it.

At a time when the last vestiges of Roman civilization
had disappeared from northern and middle Europe, when
Asiatic hordes threatened to extinguish all that remained
of occidental culture, good tidings sprang up, giving new
hope to an almost despairing population. Such rumors,
eagerly received in monasteries, villages, and scattered
strongholds, were usually carried by wandering bards and
storytellers. Some of their tales are preserved in local
folklore to our day, in different languages and various
poetic forms, their contents, however, amazingly alike.
Probably dating back to the eighth century, their message
was that a man at last has appeared on earth whom God
has found worthy of serving the Holy Grail. The new king
of the Grail, surrounded by a chosen brotherhood of
disciples, was revered under different names, but the

legends seem to refer to one and the same person. In one of the most significant Grail stories of the thirteenth century, ascribed to Albrecht von Scharfenberg, he is called Titurel. The new castle of the Grail, built by Titurel and totally inaccessible to the profane, may well have been no more than an outwardly unpretentious stronghold for knights and monks somewhere in the cave-riddled, forbidding mountain ranges of the Pyrenees.

It is this story of the second coming of the Grail that is the basis for Richard Wagner's opera, *Parsifal*. Wagner, too, has given the name of Titurel to its first, deeply revered leader, under whose long reign the knighthood of the Grail flourished, again creating secondary centers. Apart from England, where the order left an indelible memory, its better-known outposts existed along the river Rhine, in Thuringia, Switzerland, Yugoslavia, Carinthia, and southern France. Some prominent figures of the Church, like Alcuin, Charlemagne's chief adviser, Hrotswitha of Gandersheim, and somewhat later Elisabeth of Thuringia and Nikolaus von der Flue, were persistently linked by folklore to the order of the Grail.

In Richard Wagner's drama, Montsalvat, the castle of the Grail, harbored during the long reign of Titurel not only the sacred chalice but also the holy spear, whose point, according to Robert de Borron, was fashioned from the blade that had pierced the side of Christ on the cross.

Through the Middle Ages the chalice and the spear, together with the cross, represented the most sacred objects of Christian faith. Like all true relics, they were considered incentives to meditation on man's quest for ultimate truth, as well as dispensers of grace. In the preceding chapters on the Ring cycle, the importance that the symbol of the spear held already in pagan times has been pointed out. Gods like Wotan in Germanic and Pallas

Athene in Hellenic mythology were marked by the symbol of the spear as caretakers of divine wisdom and wielders of the tremendous power that knowledge of cosmic and natural laws confers.

In the opera *Siegfried*, the shattering of the sacred spear in Wotan's hand by the young hero's sword represented the awakening power of man's independent thought and will. Like the sword, the spear also represents the thrust of light in its eternal struggle against darkness. But the hilt of the sword ends in the human fist; the long shaft of the spear reaches beyond the hand of its wielder. When the spear was shattered and the reign of the immortals ended in the twilight of the gods, ancient wisdom disappeared from the earth. But Christian mysticism saw in Christ's incarnation the descent of God to earth: "And the Word became flesh." The spear of wisdom, a useless shard in the hands of mere mortals, could be restored only by the sacrifice of Christ. Thus the lance that had pierced His side became the archetype of a new wisdom within reach of man, to be used or misused by him, depending upon what he did with the awesome gift of his free will.

Where there is light, there is also darkness. Near the castle of the Grail lives Klingsor, a man possessed by a burning desire to become a knight of the brotherhood. Yet instead of following the long weary road of self-purification, he attempts to reach this goal by a violent act against nature. Unable to control and eventually sublimate the desires of the flesh, he emasculates himself and thus removes the challenge without which victory cannot be won. When Klingsor learns at last that his act against nature, far from opening the gates of Montsalvat, has actually barred them forever, his longing turns into hate. He is now determined to seize by force what he no longer can obtain by grace.

Wagner draws here a highly significant parallel between Alberich's greedy quest for the Rhinegold and Klingsor's fanatical pursuit of the Grail. The gold of the Rhine as well as the Grail relic represent creative forces left to the earth through an act of divine sacrifice. The Rhinegold is the power capable of perfecting the earth's imperfect state of biological evolution, the Grail the power capable of transubstantiating matter into spirit. The former is a gift of the Father, the latter of the Son.

Alberich, in search of love, stumbles on the secret of the Rhinegold. When its guardians reject his crude advances, he gains temporary possession of the gold by forswearing spiritual love. Klingsor, through his act of self-emasculation, tries to gain access to the Grail by forswearing biological love. Although the Rhinegold and the Grail represent the most potent remedies for man and his planet, they can be turned into deadly poison when they fall into evil hands. For so great is the Creator's love for His creatures that He has left part of His own substance at their mercy. And freedom, the highest gift He can bestow, means non-interference in man's ultimate choice between good and evil.

Brunnhilde's sacrifice has restored the Rhinegold to depths where, for a while at least, it will be safe from greed and the lust for power. The Grail, however, is guarded by mere men of flesh and blood, corruptible and vulnerable as all men are, even the greatest. Close to the sanctuary of light, Klingsor builds a sanctuary of darkness, the magic stronghold of the Antigrail. From there he endeavors to corrupt the knights of the Grail. When too many of them turn traitors and join Klingsor's forces, Amfortas, Titurel's successor, sets out to vanquish the stronghold of the Antigrail.

What the young, impetuous king fails to see is that

Klingsor's success is possible only because the knights of the Grail are once again weakening in their spiritual dedication. Instead of fighting the battle against evil in his own domain, Amfortas takes up arms to destroy its chief representative on earth. But the power of evil cannot be conquered by arms alone. And Amfortas compounds his error by taking into battle the holy spear itself.

Here Wagner points to one of the tragic errors so often repeated in human history. This error occurs whenever spiritual leaders, in defense of their cause, good as it may be, rely on divine help without being pure enough to deserve it. And whenever they fall victim to spiritual pride, average man — for whose salvation they believe they are fighting — tends to join forces with their opponents. In the opera *Parsifal*, Kundry represents average man, and it is her alliance with Klingsor that vanquishes the king of the Grail. Amfortas, well prepared to face the monsters of hell, finds himself confronted instead with the irresistible charm of eternal Eve. Forearmed against the darkness of Satan, he is defenseless against Lucifer's dazzling light. His suppressed but never fully sublimated desires make him an easy victim of temptation; and now, no less a sinner than those he had presumed to redeem, he betrays his mission. He can no longer guard the sacred weapon, the symbol of divine wisdom. The holy spear falls into Klingsor's hand.

Klingsor's victory over Amfortas signifies more than the decline of the spiritual power of the followers of the Grail; it forebodes a fateful change in man's consciousness. The knowledge of natural and cosmic laws, thus far withheld by a small group of sages from the still immature intellect of the masses, becomes gradually separated from the atmosphere of compassion, wonder, and reverence that alone could have made it an instrument for true human progress. Applied in a merely intellectual and materialistic fashion, it gives birth to an era of corrupted science that mistakes any kind of knowledge for wisdom and even the most meaningless technological inventions for progress.

Between the worlds of the Grail and the Antigrail stands Kundry. Her name appeared previously in Wolfram von Eschenbach's epic poem, and probably dates back to much earlier legends. In Richard Wagner's *Parsifal*, Kundry is the female representative of average man, ever vacillating between good and evil. Believing in repeated earth lives, Wagner traces Kundry's existence back to the time of Christ, when she saw Jesus staggering under the weight of the cross: "I saw Him — Him — and laughed! Then his glance met mine — now I seek Him from world to world." At times Kundry appears in the sacred district of the Grail to serve its knights, but at other times she is Klingsor's slave. It is in such a state of moral decline that she seduces Amfortas, to make him forget his mission and betray his trust.

In the trinity of Amfortas, Kundry, and Klingsor lies the clue to one of the great secrets of destiny. At all times, there have existed on earth conscious representatives of good and evil; and between them, forever vacillating, average man. It is he — so magnificently characterized also as the hobbit, in Tolkien's *The Lord of the Rings* — who holds the key to the ultimate fate of humanity. Thus, when the time of final choice arrives, it will be Kundry whose decision will give victory either to the Grail or to the Antigrail.

The knighthood of the Grail is in deep distress. Its king, Amfortas, has not only failed in his "holy war," but by his own fall and the loss of the sacred weapon has also immeasurably strengthened the power of evil. Although wounded by the spear now in Klingsor's hands, his life was saved by a desperate charge of his knights, who eventually carried him back to Montsalvat. Years have now gone by in torment, for the wound in his side remains unhealed. Yet in spite of deep remorse and ceaseless prayers, Amfortas has not been relieved of the duty that compels him to conduct the ritual of the Grail and to be priest-king to its knights.

According to Wagner and much older sources, the cup of the Grail was unveiled at certain times of the year. In its presence, the assembly was lifted to a higher state of intuitive consciousness. This state permitted the knights to gain deeper insight into the meaning of life, and to experience a renewal of spiritual strength together with an awareness of deeds to be accomplished. The bread and wine of which they partook during such celebrations were transformed by divine grace to become a wellspring of strength, reviving body and soul.

Yet the unveiling of the Grail, greatest bliss to the pure, brings unspeakable agony to Amfortas, who is tormented by the festering wound in his body and the sense of unredeemed guilt in his soul. The Grail chooses its own king, and none but he can unveil it. The knights feel deepest compassion for their king, but for reasons spiritual and personal must insist on his performing the sacred rites.

The opera begins in a mood of deep tragedy. Once again Kundry appears at the castle to bring a rare unguent to heal Amfortas' wound. To no avail, for the wound inflicted by the sacred spear can be healed only by the weapon by which it was wrought. Then, like a breath of fresh air in an atmosphere of deepest gloom, enters Parsifal, more child than man, still untouched by guilt or guile. In his youthful exuberance, he has followed the flight of a white swan and killed it with an arrow from his self-made

bow; thus he has shed blood in a sanctuary where all life
is sacred. But when Gurnemanz, first knight of the Grail,
makes the boy aware of the suffering he has caused, a
sense of deep compassion and remorse transforms Parsifal's heart: he will never kill again.

Guided by Gurnemanz, the young intruder is now
taken into the innermost sanctum, to behold the Grail
unveiled and witness the agony of its tormented king.
Gurnemanz hopes that Parsifal may be the bearer of grace
promised by the Grail. But Parsifal's spirit is still asleep,
and seemingly untouched by the glory as well as by the
tragedy of the spectacle he has seen, he remains silent.
Disappointed and angry, Gurnemanz sends him away to
continue on his thoughtless journey through life.

In his magic garden, Klingsor lies in wait for Parsifal.
He alone knows that the boy, the simpleton whom Gurnemanz has just angrily dismissed from the castle of the
Grail, is its last and only hope. Though well aware of the
dormant greatness of the youth, Klingsor puts his trust
in the seductive power of Kundry. She, protest as she may,
has become his tool again. Her flaming desires, forever
unfulfilled and thus ever more tormenting, make Kundry
dependent on Klingsor in the sense in which an addict
is dependent on the supplier of his drugs. And — so the
sorcerer reasons — what chance has Parsifal, the wholly
inexperienced and unsuspecting youth, of resisting her to
whom Amfortas, the priest-king of the Grail, has succumbed?

The opening scenes of the second act may well contain some of the most profoundly artistic expressions of
the art of seduction to be found anywhere in the world
of music and literature. In them Wagner unveils levels
of temptation reaching all the way from the most primitive
to the most sophisticated. On the first level, the youth is

met by beautiful girls, flowers turned into maidens by Klingsor's magic. These maidens had seduced many of the Grail's knights when their mission led them through Klingsor's enchanted realm. They represent the seductive power of purely biological desires. But Parsifal is Siegfried in a much later phase of evolution; as Siegfried he already has killed the dragon in his own blood, and where Siegfried triumphed Parsifal cannot fail. The flower maidens are pleasing to his eye, but their soulless beauty can no more arouse desire in him than Fafner the dragon could arouse in Siegfried the thrills of fear.

But now Kundry enters the scene. Wagner visualized her as the embodiment of all that is seductive in woman, in Eve, confronting Adam ever and again on his quest for the lost Garden of Eden. Compassionate at times, self-effacing, yearning for a guide toward a great and lofty goal, she is at other times the most deadly tool of the Serpent, compelled by nature always to test the spiritual strength of her mate. And if she finds him weak, she turns into Lilith, the merciless destroyer of flawed souls.

Kundry's attempt to seduce Parsifal, and her failure to achieve the victory that would have doomed them both, are by no means glorifications of puritanism. Wagner, as the conduct of his life and his private letters show, was decidedly no puritan. Yet he knew in his higher consciousness that no man can be great or fulfill his mission in life unless he has learned to master his passion in those crucial moments of destiny when conscience stands in opposition to desire.

The seduction scene in the second act of the opera reveals Wagner's deep understanding of all facets of human psychology. His Kundry, being all woman, knows all the secret longings in a man's heart. Thus it is possible for Wagner to give a brief lesson on the laws of seduction.

He knew that the merely physical appeal to a man's senses presents a real challenge only to the totally immature, or to the person whose juvenile sex life has remained unchanged throughout the years until eventually it has turned into the pathetic libido of the senile.

For Parsifal, the true test begins when Kundry, after contemptuously dismissing the flower maidens, calls him by his long-forgotten name. That this is not a given or family name is clearly expressed in the script itself: "So once, when dreaming, my mother called me." Wagner refers here to the youth's true identity, to the unknown eternal self hidden in every man's breast. And it is one of the mysteries of early love that it can arouse the first dim awareness of self-identity. But what takes place almost unnoticed in ordinary life is roused by Kundry, intentionally and dramatically, to bind Parsifal, "the guileless fool," with the ties of emotional dependence. In that sense, a woman loved may indeed become spiritually a mother to the youth she awakens to selfhood, but woe to both if such a relationship is permitted to lead to dependence.

Power over Parsifal, however, is exactly Kundry's aim, and it is no coincidence that the next step she takes toward this goal is to tell the youth the story of his mother's death. Forsaken by him, her only child, friendless and utterly alone, Herzeleide has died in Kundry's arms, handing over to her — or so Kundry implies — the sacred trust of caring for her son whom she had loved more than her life. Kundry's story marks the end of Parsifal's carefree childhood, awakening in his soul a deep sense of guilt and loneliness. Although he has left his mother without so much as a word of farewell, his heart has never taken leave of her. Up to this fateful moment, he has still harbored the delusion of youth, the delusion that his mother is waiting for him, and with her the security and peace of childhood, should he ever, tired of adventure, return to his abandoned home.

Kundry's tale puts an end to this dream, and, frightened of the dark realities of adult life, he seeks refuge in the arms of her who seems to offer him a new haven of childhood. The loneliness of a child who has lost his mother, the guilt of the son who has caused her death — these are the agonies that Kundry has aroused to make Parsifal seek solace from her, and forgiveness of the mother in whose name she claims to speak: "To thee now she sends benediction from above in this first kiss of love."

Yet, possibly for the first time, the temptress meets with unexpected failure. Once, Parsifal had seen the Grail unveiled, had witnessed the agony of its tortured king — and remained silent. But deep in his heart a seed had been planted, the seed of wonder at the miracle he had seen and of compassion for the tormented king. This seed has slowly grown, unknown even to himself. When Kundry's passionate kiss shatters the dream state of childhood and wakens the man in him, Parsifal's selfhood emerges. And this selfhood differs from that of ordinary men.

The goal of man's evolution is expansion of selfhood until it encompasses the world without. The seeker who hopes to achieve spiritual bliss by self-denial may well deceive himself. He, however, who becomes incapable of indulging in selfish desires while others need his help is truly human. Thus it is with Parsifal. Compassion, silently growing in his heart, has broken through the confines of self-centeredness. Amfortas, whom he had seen suffering in the presence of the Grail, has become part of his own inner experience. Amfortas' wound throbs in his own flesh, and in his heart burns the agony of the king's unredeemed guilt. And thus through the eyes of Amfortas he

sees Kundry, the temptress who has brought untold grief
to the king of the Grail and its knights. No longer does
she appear to him in the image of the protecting, all-know-
ing, every-youthful mother. Nor does he see the ravishing
beauty of eternal Eve, but the image of a lost soul con-
demned to destroy what she longs to possess.

A profound change has occurred in the relationship
between Parsifal and Kundry. Never again will she play
the role of the aggressor, of the domineering, comforting
mother, or claim to dispense absolution from guilt to a
bewildered, lonely youth. No woman wants to be stronger
than the man she loves. For it is only the weak, childish
strain in a man that compels a woman to dominate while,
deep in her heart, she longs to be guided. The laws of
logic do not rule human emotions. A woman cast in the
role of the stronger may deeply resent the weakness of
her mate even while she seeks by all means to increase
her power over him.

In Parsifal, Kundry has found at last the man for
whom every woman longs, the man for whom she does not
have to play the role of mother and temptress, the man
whom she can follow on the path toward a common
transcendental goal. Leaving all pretense aside, she reveals
to him the despair of her heart, appealing no longer to
his senses but to his compassion. It is an appeal that to
the merciful is almost irresistible. If made for a wrong
cause, it becomes the most dangerous of all temptations.

> *Just for one hour let me be one with you*
> *And then, though God and world condemn me,*
> *Atonement and redemption I shall find in you.*

Kundry has come a long way, but still has not learned that
no human being can be borne to salvation by another.
The Eve in her remembers darkly a stage in evolution

when, in the words of *Genesis*, man and woman were one. In Parsifal she finds Adam on his journey back to God. Not yet ready to follow him on her own initiative, she wants to merge with him body and soul, to lose her own identity and, with it, all moral responsibility. Parsifal knows that compassion will never let him attain his goal unless Kundry also finds redemption. But she must complete her journey alone, until in the sacred district of the Grail they meet again.

A long era in the history of human consciousness has come to a close. Taking advantage of the privilege only the great artist can claim, Richard Wagner at the end of the second act of his drama abandons the medieval, semi-historical setting of eighth century Christianity, and on the wings of genius transports us into the far future of man's endless journey of moral evolution.

In Wagner's cosmology, the beginning of this era was marked by another encounter between a man and a woman, when Siegfried, the pagan world's hero, the first representative of free man, met his soul's bride, Brunnhilde. At that time, their roles had been reversed. Brunnhilde represented womanhood in its untainted archetype. Her counterpart, Siegfried, was the embodiment of what the Teutonic races considered the supreme virtues of the truly masculine. These virtues included courage, strength, and, above all, an indomitable love of freedom. Had their union lasted, a race of men might have been born capable of leading the human race toward a more enlightened existence.

Contrary to modern concepts, a woman differs from a man in more than strictly physiological attributes. In the outer world, of course, man is the natural protector of woman. But since time immemorial, myth and legend have known that with regard to a man's emotional happiness and the preservation of his ideals, the woman ought to be the protector. Brunnhilde, Wotan's daughter, fearless guardian of heroes' souls, had been destined to become Siegfried's shield. For this, a woman's eternal mission, Siegfried lacks all understanding. His insistence on a physical union before love can have transformed his innermost being symbolizes, as indicated earlier, the tragic error of "emancipated" man.

At one time the relationship between the sexes was governed by strict religious and secular rules and by the dictates of honored custom. Wagner's Siegfried stands for the first true champion of freedom, and therefore also for the rebel against ancient moral laws. With his appearance on earth, not only the gods but also established customs and rules started to lose their grip on men. Had obedience to antiquated laws been gradually replaced by voluntary self-restraint, wisdom, and true chivalry, the relationship between the sexes, so crucial for the evolution of mankind, could have been raised to a higher level. But Siegfried, though representing the most advanced man of his era, fails to see that physical union marks the completion rather than the foundation of the bond between man and woman. And his era does not end with the twilight of the ancient gods; it continues to our day. For, according to Wagner's views, Christianity will triumph only in the far future when Siegfried has become Parsifal, and Parsifal the model for every man.

Before Brunnhilde, came Eve. She represented the feminine principle at a stage of evolution when the human mind started to turn its full attention outward, to the world of the senses. According to the legend, it was she who led Adam away from spiritual contentment toward the quest for earthly power and the actual experience of good and evil. In a much later era, the golden age of Teutonic Mysteries, the woman became the priestess of the hearth, the spiritual protectress of her husband, her family, and the home. The fire she had to guard signified more than warmth and encouragement: it signified the torch of spiritual longing which it was then her mission to uphold. Thus, while in the beginning it was the female element that drew Adam too far away from his Creator, at a later epoch the priestess of Artemis in Ephesus, the vestal virgins, and many other feminine servitors of similar cults became the guardians of man's waning spiritual heritage. At that time it was Adam in the guise of Siegfried who resisted the spiritual impulse, pulling the female element ever deeper into the world of unrestraint, sensuousness, and materialistic pursuits.

Siegfried's fall turns Brunnhilde into Kundry. Siegfried himself, representing all that is brave and free in man, yet arrogant and without compassion, becomes knight errant for any cause that dimly reminds him of a long-forgotten goal. Fighting, killing, and dying for ideals that do not really benefit humanity, the hero in man who has waged countless wars of destruction, pursued utopian ideologies, unleashed the atom, and is even now engaged in a pointless conquest of space, is Siegfried gone astray. Yet only as a seeker after the Grail can he find himself and his eternal goal. Only then can he atone for his failure and become Parsifal. With courage tempered by compassion, and lust for power transformed into love of God, man can attain the sanctum of the Grail. In its sacred district, Kundry will again find him to whom Amfortas will yield the kingship of the Grail.

To Richard Wagner, the central figures of his music dramas were by no means mere figments of imagination; they were entities experienced rather than invented, living a life of their own. Letters addressed by Wagner to his friends, dealing with the problems of Tristan's destiny, illustrate this point. He had intended that Parsifal should meet and comfort lovelorn Tristan, who was pining away in his desolate stronghold. Yet try as he might — so Wagner confesses — he could not succeed in bringing about this event. Believing in reincarnation within the world of artistic reality as well as in life on earth, he pondered the further destiny of his Tristan who had lost his life in a useless cause. Only years later did Wagner discover Tristan's troubled spirit in Amfortas — the spirit of a man great enough to become king of the Grail, but not pure enough to resist temptation.

The bond between Siegfried and Parsifal is revealed by the symbolic language of the music dramas themselves. Little imagination is required to see, in Parsifal, Siegfried returned, matured by suffering and chastened by failure. At first, the life patterns of the two heroes show unmistakable similarities. Both their fathers have died in battle; and their mothers, fleeing from violence, give birth to them in the protection of lonely forests. Sieglinde, Siegfried's mother, dies at his birth, leaving him to the tender mercies of Mime, the evil dwarf; Herzeleide is permitted by fate to envelop her child in a cloak of over-protective love. Siegfried is separated from the world by Mime's tyranny; Parsifal is kept in isolation and complete ignorance by a mother wanting him to remain her child forever. Yet neither Mime nor Herzeleide succeeds. Siegfried kills Mime in anger. And Herzeleide's death is caused by Parsifal's thoughtlessness, for when knights in shining armor pass by their forest home, the youth follows them without a word of farewell to his mother. "Her heart broken by grief, Herzeleide dies."

In Wagner's Siegfried image, the Indo-Germanic

ideal of the true hero finds its most eloquent expression. This ideal was firmly rooted in the hearts of the masses and unceasingly reiterated in the chants of storytellers, the principal teachers of ancient culture and morals. In the high age of paganism, the hero, besides being strong, brave, and merciless in battle, was also expected to attain almost puritan virtue by victory over his lower instincts. Thus Siegfried takes the first step toward becoming his era's idol by slaying the dragon that represents, among other soul qualities, all that is subhuman in man.

While Siegfried, the hero of the past, seeks mastery over his lower nature by combat and violence, Parsifal, the hero of the future, meets this crucial test in a far more subtle manner. When the ancient seer contemplated the child awakened from his innocence by the burning desire of his blood, the archetypal picture of the fire-breathing dragon appeared before his inner eye. When Wagner, who in his great moments of inspiration may indeed be called a seer, contemplates the struggle of adolescence as it may have to be fought in the future, an image radically different from the ancient picture of the slaying of the dragon arises in his mind. Thus Parsifal, when faced for the first time with the seductive power of sex, does not see a fierce dragon threatening the very essence of his soul. Instead, he innocently admires the lovely flower maidens, whose soulless beauty cannot rouse him even to a flicker of desire. The flower maidens, conjured up by Klingsor to seduce Parsifal, represent nature's inherent forces of procreation, innocent themselves but destructive when misused by man.

After Siegfried's victory over the dragon, nature reveals herself to him in her loveliest form. His heart comprehends her language when she speaks to him in the voice of her creatures, a voice that Wagner recaptures in the

magic of his forest music. To understand the language of
nature is the gateway to true romanticism, happiness,
and creativity. It expands man's selfhood to encompass the
world around him, without which he remains a lonely,
isolated creature, incapable of fulfilling his mission on
earth and blind to many dangers of which a fully developed
empathy with his surroundings would have warned him.
Siegfried as a youth was led by the voice of a bird to
Brunnhilde and to the realization of his mission. In later
years, his inner senses grown dull, he no longer understands the warning of his little friends, which, if heeded,
would have saved his life.

In Parsifal, man's understanding of nature has
reached a higher state. The Mysteries of old taught their
pupils to comprehend nature and become disciples of the
divine forces revealing themselves often through the most
humble of her creatures. The hero of the future will have
to submit to a far more difficult test. Can he, motivated
by compassion, become a savior of lesser creatures, as he
himself was saved by the compassion of a god? Parsifal
does not need a bird to lead him to his mission and protect
him from evil. After learning from Gurnemanz the sacred-
ness of all life, he comprehends nature in a much more
profound sense. To him she turns in a trust that man has
time and again disappointed by his self-seeking greed and
merciless exploitation. When after a weary journey and
untold suffering Parsifal at last finds his way back to the
sacred district of the Grail, he has matured enough to
comprehend Gurnemanz' words: "Nature cannot discern
the Savior on the cross. Thus, trustingly she lifts her
glance to man redeemed."

Richard Wagner hints here at certain secrets of
evolution. Had Siegfried, the hero of the past, not failed,
he would at best have remained nature's ward. Parsifal,

the hero of the future, must become her redeemer.

The image of Siegfried represents the emergence of free will in man, and his mastery over his own destiny. The moral laws, and the great wisdom that in very ancient times had molded pagan society, fall with the shattering of the sacred spear before the awakened self-seeking will of growing individualism. Man's newly won freedom has made him his own master, but it has also opened a chapter full of false pride and violence that has brought untold suffering to the human race. The spear of Wotan, on whose shaft were written the sacred laws of antiquity, inspires neither fear nor awe in the rebellious youth whose individual will proves stronger than the might of the gods.

In Parsifal's time, gods no longer wield the spear. Universal laws have been mastered by men pursuing selfish aims in their search for power. Thus laws once held in trust, as it were, by priests and sages, have become common knowledge in the disenchanted world of a god-estranged science. Man has become free from religious tutelage, but the price for this liberation has been high. For man has lost the gift of wonder. And the laws inherent in physics, chemistry, and other aspects of nature have become profane because they are used without mercy toward nature and without gratitude to the Creator. In Wagner's language, the spear has fallen into Klingsor's hand.

With the power inherent in that spear, the sorcerer hopes to conquer the cup of the Grail itself, the last receptacle on earth for divine grace. But as Siegfried once stood in the way of the quest by Alberich and Hagen for absolute power, Parsifal alone now stands in the way of Klingsor's evil plot. To remove this last obstacle, the magician hurls the spear at Parsifal, but its power, wielded by unclean hands, cannot harm a soul fully transformed by compassionate love. Unlike Siegfried, Parsifal does not smash the spear directed against him, nor does he use the weapon for his own protection. His only aim is to bring it back to the brotherhood of the Grail.

Thus starts Parsifal's weary quest for the Holy Grail. Many are the enemies he has to face, but he never uses the sacred weapon to defend his life. He brings the relic, undefiled, back to the sanctum of the Grail.

With the gradual change from the intuitive state of consciousness still predominant in the Middle Ages to the intellectual thought life of present times, the once instinctive understanding of the Grail Mystery has all but vanished. To the modern way of thinking, which rightly can be called brilliant in its sparkling superficiality, any attempt to deal with the legend of the Grail as a reality instead of as a trivial psychological symbol may indeed seem ludicrous. And yet the attempt must be made. For without it, the barren intellectual materialism of our age will drive our youth in ever-growing numbers into the pseudo-intuitive dream world of psychedelic drugs.

What was the true message of the Grail, the message that inspired the hearts of millions for more than a thousand years? Words can never do justice to a spiritual reality, but the following attempt to put the Grail Mystery into modern conceptual terms may help to clarify the thought life of another time.

According to ancient tradition, God's presence was once intuitively experienced by man. This primary state of consciousness was called the Garden of Eden, the Golden Age. Man, in his innate longing for moral freedom, for knowledge not only of good but also of evil, and for godlike power over a world of his own, separated himself from his Creator. Christian mysticism, whose first and probably greatest representative was the writer of the

Gospel of St. John, sees the coming of Christ as God's attempt to save man from the spiritual barrenness and ultimate self-destruction that would be the inevitable result of such separation. According to the Gospel, the Logos, the Creative Word, became Man, in order to bring light into the darkness of a God-estranged world. But "the light shineth into the darkness, and the darkness comprehended it not." Where the light was comprehended and received, however, the mystics spoke of man's redemption through the Holy Grail or, in later centuries, of a "mystical wedding" between the spirit of God and the soul of man.

In other words, the Mystery of the Grail in its profoundest sense is the spiritual renewal of man and of nature by a second act of grace. In Jesus one saw the living vessel filled with the spirit of God, thus representing the very archetype of the Grail. This new act of grace signified for the mystic of early and medieval Christianity that God was willing to give humanity a second chance by uniting His own divine substance with the substance of His creation. Since He had bestowed freedom on man, however, acceptance or refusal of the new impulse depended on man alone.

The early Christians still experienced the renewed flow of light into darkness in the sacrament, especially in the transformation of bread and wine. In the course of time, however, immediate experience faded and had to be replaced by dogma. It was then that secret brotherhoods emerged, either within or in opposition to organized religion, in the hope of training and preserving the intuitive vision once possessed by the Disciples and their immediate followers. Their heretical conviction was that the renewed flow of divine grace was dependent on man's fully conscious cooperation, and that without such cooperation

Christianity itself might fail.

If ideas like these are hard to grasp, the following will seem even more bewildering to present-day thought. Yet what may be totally foreign to most modern intellectuals may not appear irrational to a younger generation already in full rebellion against the barren concepts of a materialistic age.

Of the two main prejudices confusing the modern mind, one, carried over from nineteenth century concepts, is called emergent evolution. It seeks the wellspring of all being in matter, disregarding the fact that neither matter nor physical energy can by their very definition be self-creating. To credit the atom, or still lesser units, with the origin of the universe is infinitely more illogical than to seek in particles of paint and stone the clue to a great work of art. The second prejudice is a condescending belief on the part of our intellectuals that the scholars of old were mere neophytes on the lower rungs of the ladder leading up to present-day wisdom. In downgrading all that he no longer understands, modern man misses the fact that our civilization owes virtually all its truly creative ideas to the wisdom of the past.

The alchemists, for instance, knew about the possibility of transforming one metal into another, and they also knew that beneath solid matter, called earth in medieval chemistry, lay a cauldron of disintegration. Since the discovery of nuclear fission, this concept has been partly accepted today. What modern science is not yet willing to concede is that at the pole opposite to the mysterious realm of disintegration must exist an equally mysterious force-field of creation. If the natural process of material dissolution is speeded up, as in nuclear fission, forces are released that technology is now learning to control. Such forces will, by their very nature, be predominantly destructive. Thus man will be inevitably drawn into the danger of disintegrating his own world, unless he discovers its counterpole, the creative power active in all processes of healing and natural growth. But although the control of nuclear fission does not require high moral standards, the secrets of true creativity may well be accessible only to those prompted by the purest of motives.

In the words of medieval science, the intangible antecedent of matter was called the *prima materia* and directly linked with the Logos. The student of true alchemy, which must not be confused with the dubious craft of the "gold-maker," strove toward moral perfection. Only when he had achieved the highest form of integrity could he become an adept of the philosopher's stone and thus capable of transforming and perfecting nature. "We know that the *lapis* is not just a 'stone'," C. G. Jung says, "since it is expressly stated . . . to consist of body, soul and spirit; moreover, it grows from flesh and blood. . . . "The Stone like the Grail is itself the creative vessel, the elixir vitae."[13]

By pointing out the relationship between the philosopher's stone and the chalice of the Grail, Jung, the tireless explorer of mystical writings, sheds light on one of the most significant mysteries of alchemistic philosophy. The alchemists believed that the blood of Christ, the *Sang Real*, was the only matter on earth wholly permeated and transubstantiated by the power of the Creator. Thus it was itself the true philosopher's stone, which, when it came in contact with such base metals as the point of the lance and the chalice, transformed them. If modern terms are permissible, one might speak of a chain reaction of transubstantiation, as contrasted with the chain reaction of nuclear disintegration. This course of a new creative act started with the holy blood, the *Sang Real*, transforming the chalice into the Saint Graal, in whose presence on earth one saw a divine pledge that man, and eventually all nature, may still be lifted to a higher state of existence.

Two forces face each other across the world of matter. One tends to draw the earth down into a cauldron of disintegration; the other has the power of transforming it upwards. Man, having wrested from the gods the spear of power, the knowledge of natural laws, must set the course he and his world are going to take. Whatever delusions we may still nurture about so-called progress, in the end science will serve only total good or total evil. It will either redeem the world or destroy it, depending on the source whence man receives his inspiration: Grail or Antigrail. If, as Wagner hopes, Parsifal and Kundry, the Adam and Eve of the future, will open their hearts to the Grail, they will not only save themselves and the world, but also redeem from His voluntary bondage Him who has sacrificed part of His substance for love of man. It is this possibly most profound of all medieval concepts that Wagner uses in the magnificent finale of his work: "Miracle of highest grace: Redemption for the Redeemer."

APPENDIX

Narrative Reductions of the Operas
by M.G.H. Gilliam

In most English synopses the complicated plots of the *Ring* cycle and *Parsifal* are inadequately summarized. For this reason, and to offer the reader a ready reference, narrative reductions of the five librettos follow as an Appendix.

The Rhinegold

Scene i

In the twilight depths of the Rhine, three beautiful
Rhine Maidens playfully dart to and fro as they guard the
sacred treasure of their domain, the Rhinegold. Soon
Alberich appears from a dark chasm, attracted by their
merry movements. When they catch sight of him, they
retreat, distrustful of the dwarf. Alberich cheerfully cries
out that he does not mean to disturb their games; he merely
wishes to join in, and begs them to come close and play
with him.

The Maidens perceive that he is set on flirting and
their fears vanish. One by one they taunt him, first leading
him on, then jeeringly rejecting his advances. When he
sees that he cannot seduce the Maidens, he decides to
capture one of them by force. But his awkward pursuit is
no match for their agility in the water. Angry and exhausted, he gives up the chase.

Suddenly a warm yellow glow breaks upon the scene.
Emerging from a point high in a central rock, it gradually
becomes a brilliant golden light whose rays shimmer
through the water. The Maidens, remembering their duties,
sing to it rapturously. Alberich's eyes are riveted to the
source of the light. At last he asks what it is. The Maidens
tell him of the "wondrous star" of golden ore that brightens
the watery depths, bringing happiness to all who bathe
in its glory.

Scornfully the dwarf questions the value of such
gold if it creates no more than a shimmering playground.
The Maidens chide him for his lustful nature and reveal
the Rhinegold's true powers. He who fashions a Ring from

this gold can gain measureless might and rule the world. But only he who forswears all love can learn how to forge the Ring. Innocent of their betrayal of an ancient secret, the Maidens laugh together. For surely the lovesick Alberich would be the last to make this sacrifice.

Greedy for power and eager for revenge against the cruel mockery of the Maidens, the dwarf scampers to the top of the rock. He angrily renounces love forever, and with great force and determination, tears the gold from its rocky home. Amid the clamor of the Rhine Maidens, he hastily descends and disappears in the darkness below. They dive after him. Lashing waves cover the lower regions with darkness, as Alberich's hollow laughter echoes behind.

Scene ii

The watery depths give way to clouds, which gradually clear to reveal an open space on a mountain top. On a distant cliff stands a majestic, turreted castle. The Rhine flows through a deep valley separating the castle from the mountain top where Wotan, king of the gods, and Fricka, his wife, lie sleeping. As Fricka awakens, the dawn's light strikes the distant castle and catches her eye. She rouses Wotan, who is still dreaming of the magnificent fortress he has bargained with earthly giants to build for him. He can hardly believe that his dream has been realized, and in such matchless splendor!

Fricka reminds him of the price he has agreed to pay the giants, for in his bargaining, Wotan promised to give them his wife's own sister, Freia. He tries to reassure Fricka by telling her that he never intended to make such a payment but used the ruse only to lure them into building the castle. His lack of concern does not satisfy Fricka; she warns that those who become greedy for power no longer see what is right and good. Wotan insists that he would never gamble with a woman's worth. Had he not prized Fricka so highly that he lost one eye fighting to win her as his bride?

Now Freia appears. She rushes to Wotan and begs him to save her from the pursuing giants. Wotan looks about anxiously for Loge, the god of fire, whose cunning may devise an acceptable ransom for her. As the giants are seen approaching in the distance, Freia turns to her brothers for help, only to find they are hiding, ashamed of having agreed to Wotan's bargain.

The giants, Fasolt and Fafner, enter. During the gods' slumber, they have toiled mightily to build Valhalla. Now they have come to collect their wage. When Wotan feigns ignorance, and asks their price, they are quick to reply: the price that was agreed upon is Freia. The giants must be mad, Wotan answers, not to have perceived that he was jesting when he offered them the lovely goddess. They berate Wotan, who with his wisdom and power is supposed to uphold treaties among gods and men. Fasolt warns him:

> You, son of light,
> Careless in matters of honor,
> Hear and beware:
> Uphold the treaties you make,
> For all that you are
> You owe to such treaties.
> Limited is your might,
> Well defined and precise.
> Wiser than we are,
> You have bound us to peace;
> But if you do not honor
> The treaties you have made,
> Peace will be ended
> And your wisdom cursed.
> This say I, a stupid giant.
> Wise though you be,
> Take it from me.

Fafner acknowledges that the gods will age and grow pale when they lose Freia; the golden apples only she can

grow give her kin eternal youth and beauty. But a bargain
is a bargain. The giants and Wotan argue heatedly. Freia's
brothers, Froh and Donner, join in, and the tone becomes
more violent. Wotan sets his spear between the adversaries. Force shall gain them nothing, he says, and indicates that he will honor his agreement.

At this moment, Loge rushes in. Wotan turns to
him for help in settling the dispute and saving Freia. Loge
has just returned from examining Valhalla, and has found
it firm and sound. He tells the gods, to their distress, that
although he had agreed to seek a ransom for Freia, he had
not guaranteed that he could do so. Her kinsmen, who
have never liked Loge, threaten him, but Wotan parts the
new adversaries and urges the gods to be patient and wait
for Loge's counsel.

Loge describes how he has searched the ends of the
earth for a ransom that will satisfy the giants. What does
man hold dearer than woman's beauty and worth, he asked
in vain. Laughter always answered him. In the realms of
water, earth, and air, woman and love were deemed life's
greatest treasures. He has heard of only one being willing
to relinquish love: Alberich, the Nibelung dwarf, who did
so for the sake of gold. It was the Rhine Maidens who told
Loge of this and begged him to seek Wotan's justice that
they might regain their treasure.

Fafner and Fasolt ask why Alberich coveted the gold.
What is the secret of its power? Loge answers that he who
fashions a Ring from the Rhinegold masters the world.
And this Ring Alberich has made. Wotan and the other
gods are seized with a desire to own it, and decide to gain
it for themselves. But Fafner and Fasolt also recognize
the gold's power; they offer to exchange Freia for it when
the gods capture the Rhinegold from Alberich. Meanwhile, they carry Freia away.

As Freia leaves, a mist rises and grows denser. The
gods begin to age rapidly. Knowing that Freia's loss means
the end of their immortality, they vow to capture the gold.
In spite of Loge's entreaty that Wotan return the treasure
to its rightful owners, the Rhine Maidens, Wotan resolves

to descend to the Nibelung's realm with Loge and take the gold for the gods' own use. As they depart, a sulphurous vapor closes behind them. It disperses gradually, to reveal a dark rocky terrain. The clamor of dwarfs at their anvils rings from a subterranean cavern where Alberich and the Nibelungs dwell.

Scene iii

Alberich drags his dwarf brother, Mime, from a cliff and threatens him with a beating if he does not hurry and finish his delicate work. Mime has been ordered to forge a special helmet from the Rhinegold that can transform its bearer or make him invisible. The frightened dwarf Mime shows Alberich his work but says that it is still not quite finished. Impatient, Alberich decides that it is acceptable as is, and hastily places it on his head. Upon his command, "Night and fog hide me now!" he vanishes in a column of vapor. To test his invisibility, he sneaks behind Mime and rains blows on the unsuspecting and bewildered dwarf. Satisfied with the helmet's extraordinary magic, Alberich utters a second command that causes him to reappear as quickly as he had vanished. Then he hurries off to attend to other work.

Wotan and Loge descend from regions above. They come upon Mime, who is crouching on the ground and whimpering. When they ask what is wrong, he confesses that Alberich, with wicked craft, has made an all-powerful Ring from the Rhinegold. Through its magic spell, he has enslaved the Nibelungs who must now work incessantly to create hoards of trinkets and magical objects. Mime also reveals that he was instructed to forge a magic helmet that he had hoped, when finished, to keep for himself. Had he been able to do so, he might have overcome Alberich's power by outwitting him at his own game. But before he could discover the helmet's true magic, Alberich forced it from him, thus adding to his tremendous powers.

Wotan and Loge assure Mime that they wish to save him and his kin. In the distance, Alberich can be seen

directing a procession of dwarfs laden with gold and silver
jewelry that they pile before him. With his helmet tied at
his waist, he shouts commands to the weary Nibelungs.
When he sees Wotan and Loge, he chases Mime back to
the work crews, and warns the intruders to leave the area.
The gods explain that they have heard of the Nibelungs'
mighty land and the dazzling riches assembled under
Alberich's rule; hence they have come to look upon these
wonders.

Alberich brags of his new-found power and haughtily
warns of the gods' downfall. "The gold I gain," he declares,
"will win me rule of the planet."

> *With my golden grip*
> *I will capture the gods!*
> *As I have forsworn love,*
> *So, too, will all that live.*
> *Ensnared by my gold,*
> *Gold alone shall you thirst for!*

When Wotan and Loge challenge Alberich's power,
he boastfully demonstrates it by changing into a giant
serpent. The two gods pretend to be impressed but challenge him to the more difficult feat of transforming himself
into something much smaller than his actual size. Rising
to their bait, Alberich changes himself into a toad. At Loge's
direction, Wotan quickly puts his foot on the toad and cap-
tures it while Loge removes the magic helmet from the
creature's head. Alberich returns to his normal shape.
Before he can escape, the gods tie him and drag him to a
shaft through which the three mount upward out of sight.

Scene iv

Loge and Wotan return to the heavens with their cap-
tive who demands to be set free. The two gods tell him they
will consider his request in exchange for the hoard of the
Rhinegold. Although Alberich is loath to agree, he does
so, thinking he will be able to keep the helmet and Ring.
Loge releases the dwarf's right hand. When Alberich

raises the Ring to his lips and murmurs a command, the Nibelungs begin to ascend from below, laden with the treasures of the hoard.

The dwarfs stack the golden objects piece by piece. When the work is complete, Alberich asks Loge to return the helmet. Loge refuses and adds it to the priceless store. Alberich now demands his freedom but Wotan withholds it, insisting that the dwarf must still surrender the Ring on his finger. When he refuses, Wotan forcibly removes it. Alberich, raging with anger, accuses Wotan of fraud and deceit. He explains that the price he paid for the Rhinegold and the Ring was a sin that he alone committed, but warns that if a virtuous god sins, he sins against all. As Loge releases Alberich, the furious dwarf curses the Ring and all those who might ever seek and hold it.

> *As through a curse came the Ring,*
> *So cursed be it henceforth!*
> *Its gold once gave me*
> *Limitless power;*
> *Now let its magic*
> *Bring death to its bearer!*
> *Let no one rejoice,*
> *Possessing the Ring,*
> *No happy eye*
> *Behold its fair gleam.*

He scuttles down the cliff, leaving a thick vapor behind him.

Fricka, Donner, and Froh gather around Wotan and Loge and rejoice at the sight of Freia's ransom. From afar, Fasolt and Fafner approach with Freia between them. The gods' youthful appearance begins to return. The giants arrive and express their reluctance to give up Freia, explaining that to part from her radiance will be possible only when she is no longer in their sight. As the measure of her ransom, they demand that the gold be so piled as to hide her. They thrust their staffs into the ground on each side of her to mark her height and breadth while the gods begin to stack the hoard within the markers. When they reach the designated height, they stop. But the sheen of Freia's hair still shows above the gold, and Fafner demands that Loge add the helmet to the heap. Reluctantly he does so. Fasolt inspects the massed treasure and discovers a small hole through which he still can see Freia's starry eyes. This opening must be filled; otherwise he cannot bear to part with her. As the only object remaining to the gods is the Ring on Wotan's finger, the giants demand that it too be placed on the heap. Wotan refuses.

Loge reminds Wotan that he has promised to restore the magic Ring to the Rhine daughters. But Wotan answers that he intends to keep it as his reward for winning the hoard from Alberich. The giants angrily pull Freia from behind the hoard and start to leave. As Wotan holds back in spite of the gods' pleas, the scene darkens, and Erda, the Earth Mother, appears. Stretching out her hand in warning, she urges Wotan to yield the Ring and flee its curse. Slowly she sinks back into the earth and disappears before Wotan can question her.

Wotan gazes thoughtfully before him, then throws the Ring upon the precious pile and demands Freia's return. She hastens toward the gods and they embrace joyfully. Meanwhile, Fafner has opened a sack and begun to sort and pack the hoard. Fasolt observes his greedy actions and tries to stop him, asking the gods to see that all is divided fairly between them. While Wotan turns away contemptuously, Loge advises Fasolt to let Fafner take what he will and to keep only the Ring for himself. But Fafner refuses to give it up and the two giants begin to fight. With a stroke of his staff, Fafner kills Fasolt, wrests the Ring from his brother's dying grasp and throws it into his sack. For the first time, Wotan realizes the horror of the Ring's curse, and the dreadful price he has paid for his castle.

Donner mounts a rock and calls on the forces of nature to clear the mists that still hover in the air and hide the gods' new abode. A heavy stroke of his hammer causes lightning to flash; a tumultuous thunderclap follows. The clouds disperse and a rainbow bridge appears over the

valley, stretching from the mountain to the castle that
gleams in the setting sun. The gods pause in admiration;
Wotan takes Fricka by the hand and slowly leads the procession toward their new fortress. Loge remains behind
for a moment in deep contemplation. He realizes, as if by
premonition, that the gods go blindly on their way while
their reign begins its decline.

> *They hasten to their doom*
> *They, who deem themselves immortal!*
> *I feel ashamed*
> *To share in their actions;*
> *So am I tempted*
> *To change myself back*
> *Into fiery flames*
> *And consume those*
> *Who once tamed me,*
> *Rather than stupidly perish*
> *With those blind ones —*
> *Although they are gods the most godlike!*

As Loge leaves to join the other gods, the singing Rhine
Maidens can be heard from the valley below lamenting
their lost Rhinegold.

The Valkyrie

ACT I

Siegmund flings open the door to a hall built around a mighty ash tree. He glances about, then rushes inside to escape a violent thunderstorm, seeking refuge and rest. He has been wounded in a battle that he had fought single-handed against a clan of nearby inhabitants. The hall is empty. Siegmund moves to the hearth and sinks exhausted onto a bearskin rug.

Sieglinde, the lady of the abode, is astonished to find the stranger when she enters. She approaches cautiously, and discovers that he has fainted. As she bends over to examine his cuts and bruises, he regains consciousness and begs feverishly for water, which she fetches in a horn. Siegmund asks to whose dwelling fate has brought him, and Sieglinde answers that she and the house belong to Hunding. She warns that Siegmund must leave before he returns, but Siegmund assures her that Hunding will not be angry once he realizes that his uninvited guest is weaponless, wounded, and therefore harmless.

Sieglinde accepts his words. She refills the horn with a mellow mead, which she offers to Siegmund to give him strength. Who is pursuing him, she asks, and learns that it is no human enemy, but simply "misfortune." Siegmund rises and prepares to go rather than risk bringing trouble to her dwelling, but Sieglinde persuades him to stay. He remains motionless, his eyes fixed on Sieglinde's features as if trying to recall her name and face.

Hunding is heard outside; he enters armed with spear and shield. Seeing Siegmund, he stops. Sieglinde answers her husband's questioning look by telling him that the stranger has wandered in from the storm. Hunding gives his guest the customary welcome for the night, and instructs his wife to bring food and drink. While she prepares the table, Hunding scrutinizes Siegmund and is struck by the resemblance between his wife and the stranger. He beckons Siegmund to the table, bids him eat, and demands his name. Siegmund responds that he is called "Woe-king."

He tells Hunding that he was born a twin. One day when he and his strong, daring father returned from hunting, they found their lordly hall reduced to ashes, Siegmund's mother murdered, and his sister gone. Together he and his father fled to the wilds, where they lived like wolves. One day in a furious battle, his father vanished, leaving no trace but a wolfskin. Left on his own, Siegmund was drawn to towns and villages where, as an outcast, he was treated with scorn.

> *What advice I gave,*
> *Others deemed wrong,*
> *What looked evil to me*
> *Others favored as right.*
> *Wherever I went,*
> *Strife I found*
> *On all my paths.*
> *Wrath sought me out*
> *When happiness I sought,*
> *Only woe did I find,*
> *Thus "Woe-king" must be my name,*
> *For over woe alone do I rule.*

Siegmund goes on to say that he lost his weapon while aiding a young girl in distress. Her kinsmen had wanted to marry her to a man she could not love. In the bloody battle that ensued, Siegmund protected her with his spear and shield from warrior and kinsman alike. Hunding becomes grave. He was among those who answered the summons for vengence demanded by the girl's kin; now he harbors the very culprit he had sought to destroy. Honor demands that he permit Siegmund to remain as a guest in his house for the night, but Hunding warns that on the morrow Siegmund must prepare to fight.

Sieglinde is ordered to bed. She fetches her husband's nightly drink from the cupboard, then starts toward the bedchamber. Before she reaches the doorway, she pauses and turns her head toward Siegmund, who has watched her every step. She tries by her glance to direct his attention to the ash tree in the center of the hall. Noticing her hesitation, Hunding directs her to go and follows her into the adjoining room.

Alone by the dying fire, Siegmund reflects on his situation. His father had foretold that he would find a sword in his time of greatest need. His thoughts then turn from the sword to Sieglinde, whose beauty and manner have kindled love in his heart. The fire goes out, and Sieglinde slowly reenters the room and approaches him. Because she has mingled a drug with Hunding's drink, she tells Siegmund, he lies in a deep sleep. She guides Siegmund to the ash tree, from whose trunk the hilt of a sword protrudes, and tells him how it came to be there.

During the celebration of her forced marriage to Hunding, a Wanderer, clad in gray, entered the hall. His hat was pulled low over one eye; a threatening look from his other eye filled all save her with terror. The stranger carried a sword, which he swung and drove deep into the stem of the ash tree. He who can free the sword, he then proclaimed, will win it as his weapon. Many have since tried vainly to withdraw it. None save the one for whom it is intended can succeed. Sieglinde longs for this one to appear; in her heart she knows that only he can save her from her unhappy fate.

> Oh, that I might find
> That friend,
> Come from afar
> To give me help.
> The things I have suffered
> In anguish of soul,

The pain I have felt
From scorn and from shame —
Sweetest revenge would
Pay for these sorrows!
All that I lost
I would then regain;
All that I mourned for
Would then be restored.

Siegmund is moved by her tale and assures her that he is the friend for whom she waits; he is the "heir both to sword and wife."

Rapture overcomes Siegmund and Sieglinde. The outer door swings open and moonlight floods the hall; they embrace and sing of the beauty and magic of the night. Mutual memories of childhood awaken as they realize how much they resemble each other. Sieglinde gives her brother his name, Siegmund, the victorious one. Turning to grasp the sword, Siegmund commands it to bear witness to this name and christens it "Nothung" — "Needful," in memory of his father's prophesy. With a mighty tug he draws it from the tree trunk and holds it up toward Sieglinde. His feat confirms Sieglinde's feeling that Siegmund is her true love, and she rushes into his arms. In the enchanted night, brother and sister embrace passionately, as their pre-destined love breaks the bonds of discretion.

ACT II, Scene i

The gods know of the affairs of men on earth. In a wild and rocky pass, Wotan stands in warlike array with his spear in hand before his daughter, Brunnhilde. She is clad in full armor. He speaks to her about what has just taken place below and charges her to make ready for battle in defense of his earthly son, Siegmund. Brunnhilde prepares to leave, leaping exultantly from rock to rock up the mountainous terrain. Pausing on a peak, she gazes into the ravine below and spies Wotan's wife, Fricka, ascending in a ram-drawn chariot. She warns Wotan of

Fricka's rage, and leaves.

Fricka alights from her chariot and strides angrily toward Wotan. She accuses him of hiding, and of causing her great shame and distress. She has learned that Hunding and Sieglinde's wedlock has been violated by Siegmund as part of Wotan's plan, and reminds Wotan that she must now avenge the betrayed Hunding. Wotan asks whether the holy vow of wedlock has in truth been broken: Sieglinde has never loved Hunding, and was forced to marry him. Fricka replies that Wotan is making a mockery of the gods and of the laws he is bound to uphold. Not only does he condone adultery, but incest as well. Indeed, Wotan's own wanton behavior toward Fricka, his wife, has tarnished the sacred estate of matrimony.

Wotan explains that far more is at stake than the breaking of marriage laws. What he seeks is the creation of a man free from divine laws and divine protection, yet who freely aspires to the same goals as the gods. Fricka points out the folly of his efforts. By arranging to have Siegmund and Sieglinde fall in love, and by ordaining the sword for Siegmund alone, Wotan has destroyed the freedom he seeks to bestow. She repeats that his first and foremost duty is to uphold the law, and forces him to forswear his protection of Siegmund. Wotan most reluctantly agrees to countermand his order to Brunnhilde, and to assure that Siegmund falls to Hunding.

When Fricka departs, Brunnhilde returns to Wotan, who is gloomily reflecting on the outcome of his experiment. He confides that long ago, when the delights of young love had vanished, he was filled with a longing for power. Because of his ambition, he sometimes unintentionally entered into false contracts. He tells her the story of the Rhinegold, and admits that he has brought Alberich's curse on the gods by stealing his Ring and relinquishing it to the giants as ransom for Freia, instead of returning it to its rightful owners, the Rhine Maidens. Warnings of his doom have come from Erda, Mother Earth. To learn more of his impending fate, Wotan descended to the earth's womb. There, he won Erda with love's magic; as the fruit of their union, she bore him nine Valkyries, Brunnhilde and her sisters.

To prevent the ignominious downfall of the gods, Wotan has set the Valkyries the task of finding fallen heroes and bringing them to Valhalla to protect the castle and the gods from the attack of dark forces. But should the Nibelung dwarfs, led by Alberich, regain the Ring, their power would be great enough to destroy the gods. The gods must therefore recapture the Ring that the giant Fafner now possesses, but Wotan's own laws prevent him from taking it.

> *Before him,*
> *To whom I have given my word,*
> *I am powerless to strike.*
> *These are the fetters*
> *That bind me,*
> *For I,*
> *Who by treaties became master,*
> *Now by treaties am made slave.*

Erda has warned Wotan that when the darksome Alberich brings forth a son, the gods' end will follow swiftly, and the forces of darkness will prevail. It is rumored that the dwarf has already used the power of the Ring to win a woman, and in a loveless union has conceived a child.

The gods' ultimate salvation can come only from free man. Siegmund, however, is not free, and Fricka, guardian of the laws of wedlock, must be honored. Wotan therefore charges Brunnhilde to fight for Fricka; Siegmund must fall. Brunnhilde protests, but Wotan commands her to carry out his will. He starts into the mountains. Brunnhilde ponders her task as Siegmund and Sieglinde appear, seeking a refuge in the cave-like shelters of the rugged terrain nearby.

Scene ii

Brunnhilde hides from Siegmund and Sieglinde. Though Sieglinde urges that they move on, Siegmund restrains her, leading her to a rocky seat. In sudden panic, she tries to persuade him to leave her; she is unworthy of his powerful love. Because she has forsaken and disobeyed Hunding, she is now an outcast, and cannot bear to bring shame on her beloved brother. Siegmund assures her that his only desire is to avenge the wrong she has suffered.

Hunding's horn sounds from the distant woods, followed by shouts and the barking of bloodhounds. He has awakened from his heavy sleep; realizing that Sieglinde has broken her wedlock vows, he now pursues Siegmund. Sieglinde fears that no sword, not even a magic one, can protect them from the bloodhounds' fangs and the attacks of Hunding and his men. She shrieks at this terrifying vision, and falls unconscious into Siegmund's arms.

Brunnhilde, leading her horse Grane by the bridle, walks slowly toward Siegmund. She charges him to look at her and tells him that those who see her must soon follow her to their death. She will take him to Valhalla, where he will live with the noblest of slain heroes, with his father, and with lovely maidens who will tend him. Siegmund recognizes Brunnhilde as a messenger of the gods, and asks whether Sieglinde will go with him. When he hears that Sieglinde must remain on earth, he vows that he will not follow Brunnhilde. If she wishes a slain warrior for this day, Siegmund boasts, he will slay Hunding with his mighty sword. Brunnhilde tells him that the very god who imbued Siegmund's sword with its power has this day removed its spell. Siegmund angrily pleads for his beloved sister. He denounces the god who has betrayed him, then draws Needful and holds it over Sieglinde, preparing to take both her life and his own so that they may be together in death.

Brunnhilde is moved by his deep love. She begs him to forbear, and promises that she will alter his fate and help him in the coming battle. She hastens away into a ravine as Siegmund watches her. The distant horn calls grow louder. Heavy thunderclouds enclose brother and sister in an eerie darkness. Siegmund gently lifts the still unconscious Sieglinde onto the rocky seat, kisses her brow, and strides into the black mist that envelops the mountain peak.

The battle begins. As weapons clash, lightning flashes above the mountain crag, revealing the two warriors. Brunnhilde hovers over Siegmund, protecting him with her shield. She urges him on, but just as Siegmund aims a deadly blow, Wotan appears above Hunding in a flash of lightning and points his spear at Siegmund. Needful shatters into pieces. Hunding then buries his sword in Siegmund's breast as Brunnhilde recoils in terror. Sieglinde has awakened, to witness the deathblow. Brunnhilde hastens to her and, seating her on her horse, carries her off into the darkness.

As the mist parts, Hunding withdraws his sword from Siegmund's body. Wotan stands behind him on a rock, gazing sorrowfully at the fallen hero. He commands Hunding to go to Fricka and tell her that Wotan's spear has avenged the broken vows of wedlock. With a contemptuous gesture of the god's hand, Hunding falls dead. Wotan's reproachful words ring out: Brunnhilde must suffer a woeful fate for disobeying his orders. He vanishes amid thunder and lightning.

ACT III

On the summit of a rocky mountain stand four Valkyries in full armor. They have just arrived, bringing with them the bodies of fallen heroes. The summit is storm-swept; as lightning flashes and clouds rush by, mounted Valkyries are seen in the sky, each with a slain warrior across her saddle. The Valkyries call out as new arrivals dismount: "Ho-yo-to-ho! Hi-ya-ha!"

One by one the Valkyries reach the mountain top and speak of the heroes they have transported from earthly realms. When most of them have gathered, they check to see who is still missing. Eight are present; only Brunnhilde has not returned. They spy her coming, and see that her horse is exhausted and that she seems to be fleeing. The body across her saddle, moreover, appears to be that of a maiden, not of a man. As Brunnhilde arrives, her steed collapses. She lifts the maiden from the saddle and the other Valkyries hurry toward her. She explains that Wotan, their father, is at her heels. The Valkyries look into the distance and see a raging thunderstorm approaching from the north.

Brunnhilde begs for their help, explaining that the maiden is Sieglinde, Siegmund's sister and bride, and the earthly child of Wotan. She tells them that she defied Wotan to protect Siegmund, and rescued his bride when he fell. The Valkyries are horrified. She asks for one of their horses, but they dare not aid her.

Sieglinde regains consciousness and cries out in sorrow. She begs Brunnhilde to bury her sword in her heart so that she may join Siegmund in death. But Brunnhilde exhorts her to live, for growing in her womb is the fruit of her love for Siegmund. Sieglinde, enraptured by this revelation, now entreats Brunnhilde to save her.

The storm is nearer the mountain top and the Valkyries prepare to leave in haste. Unable to flee with Sieglinde, Brunnhilde tells her that she must go on alone. Counseled by her sisters, she directs Sieglinde eastward toward a wood in which Fafner guards the Nibelung hoard. There, he has become a dragon and lives in a cave, brooding over Alberich's Ring. This uncanny place is safe from Wotan; he avoids it at all costs. Brunnhilde assures Sieglinde that she bears in her womb the world's most glorious hero. She draws forth the pieces of Siegmund's sword, which she had collected when he fell and hidden under her breastplate. Placing them in Sieglinde's hands, she instructs her to guard them well, for he who can forge the sword anew may take the name, Siegfried — victor through peace.

Sieglinde hurries away as black thunderclouds veil the rocky heights. Wotan's voice sounds amid peals of thunder, commanding Brunnhilde to stay. She again implores her sisters, who take pity on her and agree to shield her. The furious Wotan appears before the Valkyries, who have regrouped so as to hide Brunnhilde. They attempt to calm him, but he accuses Brunnhilde of dishonoring the holiest tie of good faith by openly disobeying his command. As he accuses her of cowardice for fleeing her fate, Brunnhilde steps from behind the Valkyries and approaches her father. Her punishment, announces Wotan, she has brought upon herself. It is to be banishment from the realm of the gods. From this day forward she is to be cut off from the gods; all former bonds will be broken. Now she must lie unguarded in sleep. Whoever happens by and awakens her may take her for his own. Brunnhilde sinks to the ground with a cry. The terrified Valkyries hurry away as Wotan warns that if ever they come near Brunnhilde again, they will share her fate.

Brunnhilde tries to reason with her father and asks why her deeds are so shameful. She has merely carried out his original command, a command that he changed only at Fricka's insistence. When she appeared to the fated Siegmund, she explains, she encountered in his eyes and through his manly laments an overwhelming distress. His spirit and defiance when he learned that his divine father had deserted him kindled such compassion in her heart that she was moved to help him. Wotan acknowledges that she has done the deed he longed to do himself, but in so doing she has broken his command and thereby torn herself from his own being.

Realizing that her fate is sealed, Brunnhilde pleads with her father. If she must withdraw from Valhalla, let no unworthy man claim her from her sleep. Wotan is moved by her supplication and reminded of his great love for this glorious child. He agrees to girdle the rock on which she is to sleep with flames so terrible that none but a fearless and free being — "one freer than I, the god" — can gain access to her. Brunnhilde throws herself into Wotan's arms in gratitude. As he reflects upon his love for her and bemoans losing her, he kisses her godhead away by touching both her eyes with his lips. She sinks into a deep sleep. Wotan bears her tenderly to a low mossy bank. Gazing on her features one last time, he closes her helmet's visor, then covers her with her shield.

Pointing his spear toward the mighty peak, Wotan commands Loge to surround Brunnhilde with fierce fire. He strikes his spear point three times against the rock. A sea of flames springs up and encircles the peak. Wotan gazes at the flames, then disappears amidst them.

Siegfried

ACT I, Scene i

Mime sits alone in a rocky cave working at his forge. In despair he hammers on a sword, then stops. As he studies his work he recalls that every sword he has made for Siegfried has snapped like a toy as soon as it was put to the test. All his skill cannot forge a weapon mighty enough for the vigorous youth to use against Fafner, Mime's dragon foe. His thoughts turn to Needful, the one weapon that could fulfill the task. This was the sword of Siegmund, Siegfried's father. Try as he may, however, Mime knows that he has not the skill to reforge Needful. He returns to his craft almost certain that his efforts will fail.

With a lusty shout Siegfried enters. He is leading a large bear by a rope. Mocking and teasing, he coaxes the bear to chase the dwarf. Mime dodges and scampers fearfully about the room, begging to be left alone. But Siegfried refuses to call off the game until he is allowed to test the new sword. Mime scolds, and asks what he has done to deserve such cruel disrespect. Still scoffing, Siegfried answers that he would sooner befriend any animal of the forest than associate with an old misshapen dwarf. Then he snatches the sword from Mime's hands and flourishes it in the air. With a single blow he strikes the anvil and watches in disgust as the weapon splinters to bits.

The miserable dwarf cowers as the youth berates him: What sense are the fine tales of giants and dragons that inspire him to deeds of daring, if he is still unarmed? To placate, Mime offers food, only to have the bowl grabbed from his hand and tossed aside. Once more Siegfried is reproached for his behavior, as Mime reminds him of all he has done for him since he reared and nurtured him as a motherless babe — father and mother alike he has been to the ungrateful boy. But Siegfried has suspected for some time that the ugly creature is not his father. Has he not glimpsed his own splendid reflection in a forest pool? Surely his true parents were made of finer stuff. Indeed he has remained with his despised guardian only in order to learn something of his rightful heritage. He begins to speak of the fledgling birds and forest cubs who are nurtured by their own kind. Surely he, a human child, all the more deserved the loving care of a mother and father like himself! In righteous anger he grasps Mime by the throat and demands to know the truth, nor will he let go until he has heard all he wishes to know.

The dwarf, reluctant but frightened, finally confesses that he first encountered Siegfried's mother as she lay weeping in the woods near his abode. He helped her into his cave, where she gave birth to her child. Spent by her labor, she died soon after she had entrusted the helpless babe to the dwarf's care. Her name was Sieglinde. Although Siegfried has listened to every word, he is not satisfied and demands some proof that the story is true.

Mime fetches the pieces of a broken sword and shows them to the boy. These, too, were entrusted to his care by Sieglinde. With her dying breath she had explained that the sword belonged to the father of her child. This was the weapon that her hero had carried into his last and fatal battle. Excitedly, Siegfried urges Mime to reforge the pieces for him so that he may have his rightful and intended sword; then he will be able to wander from the forest, free as a bird, and make his way in the world. He insists that the task be finished before the day ends, and with a last threat to Mime hurries off into the forest.

Mime calls futilely after the boy, then returns to his smithy to ponder his dilemma. How can he keep Siegfried with him and persuade him to battle Fafner? How can he forge the fragments of the broken sword? No furnace is hot enough, no dwarf crafty enough, to fuse the pieces together. "The Nibelung's hate, toil and sweat, cannot make Needful new!" Because he is no match for Siegmund's sword, he sinks to the ground, sobbing.

Scene ii

Disguised as a wanderer, his face half-hidden by a drooping broad-brimmed hat, Wotan emerges from the woods and comes to Mime's cave. He greets the dwarf and asks for shelter by his hearth. Mime bids him be off, but the stranger insists that his wisdom and worldly knowledge will be at his host's disposal in return for a place to stay.

Many believe
Themselves to be wise
Yet are ignorant
Of what they need to know.
I invite their questions,
Then teach them my lore.

Mime declines his offer, and again urges him to be on his way. The Wanderer, ignoring the discourtesy, sits down at the hearth and proposes a bargain. He wagers his head that he can answer any three questions that Mime chooses to ask.

Reluctantly, the dwarf accepts the challenge. After careful thought, he asks: "What race dwells beneath the earth's surface?" The guest replies without hesitation that it is the dusky Nibelungs, and shows his further knowledge by speaking of the hoard once fashioned under the spell of a magic Ring.

Acknowledging the Wanderer's answer, Mime ponders deeply before asking his second question: "What race dwells upon the earth's surface?" Once again the stranger answers promptly that it is the race of giant-like men led by Fasolt and Fafner, who out of lust for the Nibelungs' riches won for themselves the hoard and the Ring. Cursed by its possession, Fafner killed Fasolt, then by the power of a magic helmet turned into a dragon to guard the hoard.

Mime accepts the answer and poses the final question: "What race dwells on cloud-covered heights?" The Wanderer tells him that the gods dwell in glorious Valhalla, and that Wotan is their king. From a branch of the World Ash this king once fashioned the shaft of a spear. Into its wood he carved the runes of a holy covenant, swearing before the High God of All to uphold all just treaties and agreements. Thus does he wield the mystical power to rule the world. The Nibelungs bow before him, and it is his word that subdues the giants. As if by accident, the stranger lifts the spear in his hand and strikes the ground. A thunderclap is heard, frightening the already confused Mime, who again acknowledges the mysterious visitor's third answer. The stranger has kept his part of the bargain; Mime is forced to admit that he may therefore keep his head.

The Wanderer points out the foolishness of such questions, but now it is Mime's turn to wager his head. Reluctantly he agrees to answer the three questions that will be put to him and prays that fortune will help him. The Wanderer begins: "What is the race that Wotan treats so harshly yet loves most dearly of all?" "The Volsungs," responds Mime, "The people of Siegmund and Sieglinde." The Wanderer approves the answer but adds that a cunning Nibelung harbors Siegfried, Fafner's destined destroyer, and plots to have the youth slay the dragon so that he can seize the golden hoard.

Next the Wanderer asks: "What is the name of the sword that Siegfried must wield to slay the foe?" Regaining his self-confidence, Mime gleefully answers: "Needful!" He recalls that Wotan thrust it deep into an ash tree, so that only one could possess it — the god's own earthly son, Siegmund.

Then follows the third question: "Who shall fashion the mighty pieces of this sword?" Suddenly Mime is terror-struck. Head swirling, he remembers that no effort he has made with hammer, rivet or solder has come close to repairing the sword. In desperation, he cries: "Who indeed can forge the sword if I, the cleverest of all smiths, am lacking the skill?"

The Wanderer reprimands Mime. When he had his chance to ask three questions, how could he have failed to ask the crucial one? Thus he has lost the wager and so forfeited his head. "He who has never harbored fear shall forge the sword," says the Wanderer, and with a farewell gesture charges Mime: "Guard well your head. For henceforth I leave its fate to the fearless one!"

Scene iii

Mime, staring into the forest, hears rustling in the bushes. Terror seizes him as his imagination conjures up the image of the dragon Fafner. He crouches behind the anvil, crying and trembling. But it is Siegfried who breaks through the thicket. He derides Mime for being so frightened and demands to see the progress of the sword, Needful. Mime timidly appears from behind the anvil. Still shaken and confused, he confesses that he has lost his head in a wager. He also tells the boy that only he who has never harbored fear will be able to forge the sword anew.

Mime realizes that Siegfried knows no fear, but in order not to lose him, decides he must teach him to fear. He insists that Siegfried's mother had wanted her son to learn the meaning of all things, including fear. And indeed, he would not be ready to go into the world until he experienced it. Siegfried welcomes the new lessons, and urges Mime to begin at once. Mime explains that he must follow him to Hate Cavern at the end of the wood, where Fafner has his lair. This dragon who kills and eats his fill will surely teach him fear. Siegfried is anxious to embark on this new venture, but first demands to inspect the dwarf's work on the broken sword, for he would like to use it in his coming ordeal. Mime answers that he is powerless with the sword; only fearless hands can break its magic spell. The impatient Siegfried pushes Mime aside and grabs the pieces, determined to see whether he can himself reforge his father's weapon.

He prepares a great fire in the hearth, places the pieces of the sword in a vise and impetuously sets to work with a file. Mime, mocking his lack of craftsmanship, jumps

upon a stool nearby and watches until the sword is reduced
to slivers of steel. Siegfried puts the precious splinters in
a crucible and melts them. As he blows on the fire with a
bellows, he dreams of the conquests he will make with
his mighty sword. He pours the molten metal into a mould.
Mime, watching his every move, suddenly realizes his own
predicament. If he does not teach Siegfried to fear, he
will lose his hold over him. Yet if he does teach him to be
afraid; Siegfried will be unable to slay the dragon and
win the Nibelung's hoard for the dwarf.

After forcing Mime to tell him the true name of the
sword, Siegfried plunges the mold into a cooling pail of
water, speaking only to Needful as he works. His incredible
progress, despite his clumsy craftsmanship, unnerves
Mime. Now the dwarf can do no more than devise a plan.
Siegfried will remain fearless; he will finish the sword and
slay Fafner. When he longs for a refreshing drink, Mime
will give him a poisoned potion. Then Mime will seize the
hoard and the Ring and become the new Prince of the
Nibelungs and ruler of the world. He says to himself:

> Even Alberich,
> Who once enslaved me,
> Shall soon become
> My lowly servant.
> As Nibelung's master
> I shall be their lord.
> The despised dwarf
> Shall now be obeyed!
> For gods and heroes
> Both love the gold.

Siegfried completes the casting and honing of the
sword and cries out: "With the dying father the steel was
destroyed; the living son forged it anew!" Then with a
mighty sweep of the blade, the boy strikes the anvil, which
breaks apart and crashes to the floor. Mime falls to the
ground, terrified, as the young hero triumphantly thrusts
his noble weapon into the air.

ACT II, Scene i

It is night. Alberich is lying beside a rocky cliff in a deep forest. He looks out into the darkness toward Fafner's cave. A distant bluish light flashes toward him like a shining steed dashing to and fro in the woods. The light goes out, and the Wanderer appears. Alberich recognizes Wotan at once. Calling him a villanous trickster, he charges him to be off. What more can the god want of him after taking his gold? He reminds him that he, Alberich, has cursed the golden treasure, and when he regains it he will use its power to destroy Valhalla. Whatever the Wanderer's intentions, the dwarf mistrusts them, for he knows that Wotan's blood flows in a young mortal who may be able to pick the fruit forbidden to Wotan himself.

The Wanderer warns Alberich that he should rather fear his own brother, Mime. Even now he is approaching with someone who can slay Fafner. In turn the god suggests that if Alberich informs Fafner of the dangerous plot against him, the dragon may give him the Ring as a reward; he calls out at once to awaken the sleeping beast. Alberich walks cautiously to the cave, shouts the warning and asks for the Ring as payment for saving Fafner's life, but the dragon takes little notice, and returns to his slumber.

The Wanderer laughs aloud at Alberich's failure and, cautioning him once more of his brother's intentions, vanishes into the woods. The angry dwarf curses the god and his kind, and slips into a rocky cleft nearby. Dawn breaks.

Scene ii

Siegfried and Mime enter a clearing near the dragon's cave. They sit down beneath a lime tree and ponder the strange surroundings. Now that Siegried is certain that Mime is not his father, he is determined to have nothing more to do with him. He orders him to be off, but Mime remains to give counsel. He describes the dangers of the dragon: Venom pours from his slavering mouth, and his serpent's tail lashes out and coils about his victims to crush them. These warnings serve only to stir Siegfried's enthusiasm for battle. Finally Mime instructs him to go to a nearby spring. When the dragon comes for his morning drink, Siegfried will be able to sneak up from behind and slay him. The unrelenting youth is the more determined to be rid of Mime. Despite his insistence that he may still be needed, the dwarf is insulted anew and driven off into the woods. As he leaves, Mime utters his wish aloud that Fafner and Siegried will slay each other.

Siegfried settles back happily under the tree, reflecting on the newfound knowledge that he is not related to the hated dwarf. His thoughts turn again to his own father and mother. As he tries to imagine what they would have been like, he is distracted by a bird in the tree above him. He listens to its song and longs to know what it is saying. If he imitates the melody, he may learn more of its meaning. He makes a reed pipe and so tries to match the high clear notes. His efforts are in vain. In despair he flings the pipe from him, takes his silver hunting horn, and blows a single blast upon it.

The loud and piercing sound attracts Fafner, who emerges from his cave and breaks through the underbrush. Siegfried looks at him with astonishment. Jovially he greets the dragon, showing his pleasure in this new encounter. When Fafner demands to know who he is, Siegfried parries with the challenge: Teach me fear! He exorts the beast to beware. Should Fafner fail, he must forfeit his life. The great dragon laughs at this brazen impudence, and opens his jaws to show his fierce teeth. Siegfried is uncowed; the teeth are too beautiful for such an ugly brute, he declares. What is more Fafner's jaws are open too wide. The dragon retorts that his teeth are just right for eating Siegfried, but the young man answers that he has no intention of becoming his breakfast. "Take care, old loud mouth!" he admonishes and draws his sword for the charge. Fafner snorts fire, but Siegfried dodges the spewing flames. When Fafner lashes out with his tail, Siegfried stabs it with his sword. Rearing up with an ominous roar, Fafner bears his breast and Siegfried seizes the opportunity to plunge the sword deep into the dragon's heart.

The young hero jumps from beneath his victim just before the giant body falls to the ground. In a hushed voice, Fafner asks who has vanquished him. Siegfried confesses that he knows little about himself, but admits that the dragon has roused him to anger. As the life ebbs from him, Fafner tells Siegfried that he and his brother, Fasolt, fought over the cursed Nibelung gold and that he slew his brother and changed himself into a dragon to guard it. He warns:

> *Guard yourself well,*
> *Blossoming hero!*
> *For he who enticed you blindly to act,*
> *Makes ready his plan*
> *To bring about your death.*
> *Mark my word!*
> *Watch how it ends!*

With a final groan, Fafner rolls on his side and dies.

When Siegfried draws his sword from Fafner's breast, the dragon's blood, burning like fire, spatters his hand. In an involuntary gesture the boy sucks his fingers and swallows the fiery liquid which sends an immediate burning sensation throughout his whole being. Staring in mute astonishment at the dragon corpse, Siegfried is aroused by the clear notes of the wood bird. As he turns his attention to the song, the inner burning is transformed into a new sense of awareness. Realities of the world about him are expanded and illumined by an inner light, and he hears the hidden meaning of the bird's song. He is telling him of the many treasures of the Nibelung hoard, hidden within the cave. Of all these there are two the young man should claim as his own. He should master the magic helmet and place the Ring on his finger. Properly handled, these will make him lord of all the world. Siegfried thanks the wood bird and descends into the cave.

Scene iii

Mime sneaks timidly through the forest clearing and sees that the dragon is dead. Meanwhile Alberich appears from a crevice in the cliff opposite and watches his adversary as he approaches. Alberich jumps forward to block Mime's way. In an angry confrontation, each accuses the other of trying to steal the Rhinegold and each swears that the other shall never attain the magic helmet or Ring. Then they dash off into the woods in opposite directions.

Siegfried observes his booty thoughtfully. Though he has not understood its true worth, from the friendly bird's instructions he decides that such tokens might serve as a reminder of this fair and fateful day. Hastily he hangs the helmet from his girdle and puts the Ring on his finger. The bird has followed and counsels him now to beware of Mime. He must not trust the dwarf. The blood that Siegfried tasted was charmed; now he has the power to read the villainous mind and perceive its true intent.

Soon Mime appears. He greets the young victor with flattering gestures and praises his valor and skill. His prattle is friendly enough but his words miraculously betray the dwarf's crafty plan to kill him. When Mime offers him the drink, assuring him of its healthy effects, its deadly potency is understood at once by Siegfried. Baffled by the young man's mysterious perception, the enraged Mime tries to force him to drink. But Siegfried, filled with loathing, wields his powerful sword and kills the dwarf with one fierce blow.

Alberich can be heard laughing in the distance, for he has observed what has taken place. Siegfried picks up Mime's body and throws it into the cave. Then with a mighty effort he pushes the corpse of the dragon across the entraceway to seal off the cave entirely. He returns to the lime tree, and stretches out to cool the feverish blood that now pounds through his vigorous young body. Once more the bird sings to him, telling him that he may soon take a wondrous and beautiful wife. This maiden lies sleeping high on a mountain rock, surrounded by fire. Only he who can penetrate the wall of fire and awaken her can claim her for his own.

As the song continues, Siegfried feels a new stirring in his breast. His heart beats happily with thoughts of love. The bird reminds him that only he who is fearless can break through the flames and claim the fair maid for his bride.

Siegfried answers:

> *This very day*
> *I tried in vain*
> *To learn fear from the dragon.*
> *Now I long*
> *To learn it*
> *From the maiden surrounded by fire.*

The bird flutters over Siegfried's head, bidding him follow as it guides him toward the sleeping Brunnhilde.

ACT III, Scene i

A violent thunderstorm rages. As it subsides, a flash of lightning reveals the base of a mountain. Wotan, still dressed as the Wanderer, enters and walks toward a cavernous opening in a large rock. His magical song calls forth Erda, the Mother of Earth and Primeval Wisdom. The cavern begins to glow with a bluish light and gradually Erda rises from her slumber in the center of the earth, covered with a shimmering gray-white frost. She demands to know why Wotan has awakened her. He answers that in her dreaming is boundless knowledge; he has called her to ask counsel.

Erda protests that Wotan's sisters, the Norns, are already awake and are even now spinning all knowledge into their eternal rope. Why not ask them to read from it the thoughts of Erda? But Wotan knows that the Norns weave only that which is destined. They cannot answer, as can the Mother of Wisdom, how one may stop a wheel that is already in motion.

Erda questions him again. Why does he not ask Brunnhilde, their Valkyrie daughter? She too has great wisdom. Wotan explains that she has disobeyed him and been punished by a sleeping spell that can be broken only by the man who wins her as his bride. All this seems strange to Erda who cannot understand how Wotan could punish his loving daughter for doing so fearlessly what he himself had wished done. Erda longs to return to her slumber, where wisdom and order prevail. Though Wotan demands that she answer his questions, silence is her only response.

Suddenly he realizes himself that it is his own actions that have set in motion the downfall of the gods. No longer troubled by the woe he first felt when Erda revealed to him the consequences of his deeds, he says.

> *The gods' downfall*
> *Gives me no anguish,*
> *Since I willed it so!*
> *What I once resolved*
> *In wild despair,*
> *Now gladly and freely*
> *I wish to bring about.*

Wotan reflects on his earthly descendant, Siegfried, who is happy in love and free in his selfhood. It is he who will receive the god's divine inheritance; together with Brunnhilde he will be able to perform a great deed for the world. Whatever these young ones may bring to pass will be joyfully accepted by the Wanderer.

After this triumphant revelation, he bids Erda return to her endless sleep. Erda, her eyes closed, has already begun to sink into her cavern. Dawn illumines the world and the storm ceases.

Scene ii

The Wanderer is again in a rocky terrain, resting with his back against a large boulder. He spies the wood bird leading Siegfried toward him. The fluttering bird draws near, then darts away and vanishes. Siegfried approaches but discovers that the bird has flown from his sight, leaving him on his own to find the sleeping place of his future bride. As he starts to push onward, Wotan stops him to ask what he seeks. Siegfried, thinking that the old man may know the way, tells him of the mountain rock guarded by a circle of fire wherein a maiden sleeps.

When the Wanderer hears that Siegfried has learned of this enchanted place from a bird, he asks mockingly how the young man could fathom its language. Siegfried answers that this magic was worked by a dragon's blood which changed him as soon as it had wet his tongue. Then he relates the story of Mime's attempt to teach him fear and how he urged him to slay the dragon. He explains that he forged a mighty sword with which he vanquished the giant enemy. But Siegfried is bound to admit that he does not know who made the pieces from which he remade the sword.

The Wanderer is amused by Siegfried, but the boy takes offense at his laughter and demands that the old man show him the way or step aside so that he can find it himself. In spite of the admonition that the youth should honor and respect his years, Siegfried advances. He looks more closely at the stranger, examines the monstrous hat that partly covers his face, and notices that one eye is missing. If this were lost through stubbornness, Siegfried warns, the other eye may be lost in the same way if he continues to hinder him! The Wanderer replies that Siegfried is looking with the missing eye into the one that "still is left me for sight." Siegfried laughs at the riddle and demands that the stranger move out of his way. The Wanderer cautions:

> *If you but knew me,*
> *Brash young man,*
> *Your scorn might*
> *Well have been spared.*
> *You, whom I love,*

All too exalted,
Do not awaken my wrath;
For if you do,
It would ruin both you and me!

The Wanderer attempts to prevent Siegfried's passage. The sleeping maid on the rock, he tells the boy, is charmed by his own might; he who awakens her breaks this might forever. He reminds Siegfried of the ferocious flames that encircle Brunnhilde; but the undaunted youth forces his way onward. The Wanderer now physically bars his way. He lifts his spear and challenges Siegfried with the words, "The sword that you swing once broke upon this shaft."

Siegfried, believing that his father's foe stands before him, prepares to take vengence. One stroke from Needful hews the mighty spear in two. A flash of lightning shoots upward toward the rocky heights, where the flames that surround Brunnhilde's rock become visible. A loud thunderclap follows. The Wanderer bends down and picks up the broken shaft of his spear. As he disappears into the darkness, he bids Siegfried, "Fare on. I cannot prevent you!" With a shout of joy Siegfried charges forward on his path. Soon he reaches the fire that has spread down from the heights, and plunges into the flames which appear to consume him as he ascends the mountain.

Scene iii

The fire has subsided, revealing a blue sky and clear bright weather. The sleeping Brunnhilde is visible on the summit of the rocky mountain. She is dressed in full armor. As Siegfried approaches, he first spies her horse beneath the spreading fir trees. Then the glistening steel of her armor begins to dazzle his eyes. He moves toward the maiden and lifts the shield that covers her. At first he mistakes her for a handsome youth, but as he loosens the tightly fitting helmet and lifts it from her head, her long curling hair falls at her side. Again he is struck by the radiant fairness of the sleeper. Realizing how difficult it is to breathe beneath the heavy armor, he gently cuts the rings and lifts the breastplate. Brunnhilde now appears before him in soft feminine garb, and he realizes after all that the sleeping figure is a woman.

Brunnhilde's beauty so overwhelms him that he sinks into a swoon on her bosom. His heart begins to tremble with anxiety: The radiance of her look may blind and overcome him. Is this what it means to be afraid? If so, he must awaken her and confront fear for the first time. He bends down and gently places his lips to hers. After a moment, Brunnhilde opens her eyes and lifts herself slowly to a sitting position as consciousness returns. She sings praises to the sun and to the light of the radiant day, and asks who the hero is who has broken her sleep.

Siegfried and Brunnhilde exchange greetings as they gaze into each other's eyes; both are filled with a growing ecstasy. They proclaim their mutual joy and their new-found friendship. Brunnhilde declares that she had always loved Siegfried and had suffered the penance of sleep to protect him from death in his mother's womb. The sight of her faithful horse, Grane, reminds her of the life she knew before falling into the deep sleep, and her armor and helmet rekindle a faint memory of her past.

Siegfried declares that the flame that shone around Brunnhilde's rock now burns within his breast. He embraces her, but Brunnhilde resists, afraid of losing the last trace of her remote divinity. Gently, Siegfried seeks to calm her as the pictures of her former life begin to fade. She looks at him tenderly and begs him not to conquer her in his passionate longing, but merely to look upon her and allow her to mirror back the picture of his beauty — that of a brave and joyous young man. Should she submit to his longing, she fears, her god-like calm will be tossed into tumult and her chastity's light into blazing passion. Her heavenly wisdom will flee, driven by jubilant love.

Siegfried clasps her in his arms. He confesses that he has failed to learn the fear she almost taught him, and that he is but the fool of his passion. Brunnhilde, submitting, prepares to lose the last memories of the radiant world of Valhalla. She bids farewell to the glistening light of the gods, and proclaims the end of their eternal race. Siegfried hails the light from the sun of earthly day, while Brunnhilde perceives the dusk of the gods enfolding them. She throws herself into Siegfried's arms and together they rejoice at the "love that enlightens," and "death that is joy."

The Twilight of the Gods

PRELUDE

On the rocky peak near Brunnhilde's fiery resting place are the three Norns, tall feminine beings clad in sombre, flowing garments. The first sits beneath a spreading hemlock; the second lies on a rock in front of a cave; and the third is seated just below the mountain peak. They are busily spinning their rope, which records the destiny of gods and men. They recall that Wotan, a valiant god, once stopped to drink at a mystical spring by the foot of the World Ash and, in payment for the power he gained from it, gave up one eye. From the World Ash he broke a branch, and fashioned it into the shaft of a spear. Thus wounded, the tree grew weaker until a blight finally killed it. The spring also failed.

As the Norns spin, the first fastens one end of the cord around the branch of the hemlock and proclaims, "No more do I weave beside the Ash; the hemlock must serve for fastening the cord." The second Norn winds the cord around a rock. "Evermore dried was the spring. Now the jut of this rock must hold my cord." The third Norn casts the end of the cord behind her, then throws it to her sisters. They continue to work, passing the rope from one to another.

According to their tale, Wotan dedicated his spear by carving on its shaft an oath to uphold all pacts and treaties. But the hero Siegfried destroyed his spear, and with it Wotan's power to fulfill his task. Then Wotan had the World Ash felled, and its boughs cut to splinters and placed around Valhalla as kindling. There the splintered Ash awaits the torch, for it is fated to start the conflagration that will consume Wotan's lofty castle. And when the flames devour the glittering hall, the gods will have reached the twilight of their era.

One day the mighty Wotan will turn to his fiery friend, Loge. Thrusting the broken shaft of his spear into Loge's flames, he will ignite it to kindle the Ash. The Norns recall Loge's past, when Wotan with the spear's magic tamed his brilliant flame and brought this elemental creature into the service of the gods. It was Loge who, upon Wotan's bidding, encircled Brunnhilde's rock with protecting fire. The Norns continue to spin the cord and knot it, singing of Alberich, the dwarf who stole the gold from the Rhine. As they sing of the Ring's curse, they notice that the stone around which their cord is wrapped has begun to cut through it. The cord breaks; with cries of alarm, the Norns exclaim that the rope of eternal wisdom marks time no more. They rush to their mother, Erda, as dawn gradually illumines the sky, concealing the distant glow of the circle of fire nearby.

Siegfried and Brunnhilde emerge from a cave-like dwelling. Brunnhilde fetches her horse Grane and leads him to Siegfried. Reluctantly, she prepares to bid farewell to Siegfried who must be off to deeds of glory. She tells him of her undying love and confesses to a slight fear, because in giving him all of her godly wisdom, she has lost her strength and maidenly might. Now she lives only to serve Siegfried, rich in love but lacking in power to work in the world herself. All that she asks is that he remember his deeds of valor to win her and the eternal love to which they have pledged themselves. Siegfried embraces her and assures her that she, Brunnhilde, is his only purpose. Her wisdom and love have made him a true man.

Siegfried prepares to leave his bride in the blessed protection of fire. He removes the magic Nibelung Ring from his hand. Placing this powerful charm on her finger, he pledges his sacred troth to Brunnhilde. In return, she offers her faithful horse Grane to bear him through all earthly trials. They bid farewell to one another, Siegfried to his radiant star, Brunnhilde to her conquering light.

He leads Grane down the rocky descent as she looks after him from on high. Soon Siegfried's horn sounds from the valley below.

ACT I, Scene i

Gunther and Gutrune, brother and sister, are seated on a throne in a great open hall overlooking the Rhine. Hagen, seated at a table before them, assures his half brother, Gunther, that his kingdom upholds the Gibichung name and that Gunther has added fame to his ancestors — in particular, to Dame Grimhilde, mother of them both. Gunther expresses his pleasure that as brothers they do not envy each other, for though he is lord and heir to the throne, Hagen is heir to the family knowledge and wisdom. Together they bring honor to the Gibichung household.

There is only the problem that Gunther is still unwed. Hagen wishes to find for him the rarest of women, and has selected none other than Brunnhilde, who remains protected by the encircling flames of her rocky home. When Gunther asks who can penetrate the fierce protective fire, Hagen tells him of Siegfried, son of Siegmund and Sieglinde. Siegfried, Hagen further counsels, is the man whom Gutrune should wed. He then recounts the hero's deeds of valor. If Siegfried could be persuaded, he could fetch Brunnhilde to be Gunther's bride, but it would require Gutrune to work a spell of enchantment. Hagen assures her that as in the past she can brew the magic drink that is needed. He lays out the plan they must follow. They have only to wait until Siegfried comes to their realm. Surely his quests will bring him to the Gibichung kingdom before long.

Hardly have these words been spoken than Siegfried's horn sounds in the distance. The brothers and sister soon spy a boat carrying a man and a horse down the river. Recognizing that the boat bears none other than Siegfried, Hagen and Gunther shout and wave their hands in order to attract his attention. The boat lands nearby and its passenger is welcomed ashore. Siegfried greets the strangers and announces that he is seeking Gunther, the mighty warrior of the Gibichung household. When he learns that he is standing before him, he acknowledges Gunther's fame but demands that he either fight or declare his friendship and his willingness to serve with him in deeds of goodness. Gunther at once assures him of his friendship. Not only is Siegfried welcome, but Gunther also pledges his land, his people, and his own limbs to the pursuit of the good. Siegfried, in turn, offers his life and limbs, and swears by his sword that they shall ever be friends, noting that he has no land or riches to add to his pledge.

Hagen questions his lack of wealth, referring to tales of Siegfried's newly won booty — the Nibelung hoard. Siegfried explains that he took none of it, for he had no need of riches. Pointing to the golden helmet that hangs from his girdle, he remarks that he kept only this useless trinket as a memento of his deed; a golden ring from the hoard he gave to his beloved. Hagen informs him that the helmet he considers worthless has in fact the power to transform him into any shape he chooses, and to transport him instantly to distant places.

Gunther interrupts to welcome Gutrune, who brings from the house a drinking horn filled with the magic potion. Siegfried takes the horn and holds it thoughtfully before him. Thinking of his faithful Brunnhilde, he drinks to her and their sacred love. He returns the horn to Gutrune and suddenly, overwhelmed by passion, is unable to master his thoughts and feelings. He sings of Gutrune's beauty and of the fiery raptures that surge through his veins.

> Ah, fairest maid
> Turn thy glance from me!
> Its radiance sears the depth of
> My heart,
> And turns my blood into a
> Stream of consuming fire!

Siegfried begs that he may be Gutrune's servant. Without taking his eyes from her, he asks Gunther if he has a wife. Gunther explains that he has no wife, for his mind is set on a maid who dwells on a rock surrounded by impenetrable fire. The words recall in Siegfried a faint memory; he repeats them hesitatingly. But soon his mind is made up. He offers to bridge the raging fire in order to win Brunnhilde for Gunther, if Gunther in turn will give him Gutrune's hand in marriage. He explains that he will conceal his true identity by assuming Gunther's form with the help of the magic helmet. The two men seal their pledge by drinking wine mixed with their own blood, thereby becoming blood brothers. Siegfried asks why Hagen has not joined in the oath, but Hagen excuses himself, claiming that his blood is not clear and noble like theirs, but sluggish and cold; it would spoil the drink.

Gunther and Siegfried prepare to embark in the boat on their trip to the mountain, leaving Hagen in charge of the Gibichung Hall. Hagen assures Gutrune that the two men will soon win Brunnhilde for Gunther, and that Siegfried will return to become her bridegroom. Left alone, he sits down at the table and reflects on the future. As his reward for these arrangements, he will win the Ring. "Sail on," he cries to the merry companions, for soon he, the true son and heir of Alberich, will be the Nibelung prince and all will serve him!

Scene ii

At the mouth of the mountain cave in which she dwells, Brunnhilde sits alone, deep in thought. As memories of Siegfried play in her head, she lifts the Ring to her lips and covers it with kisses. Thunder rolls in the distance. For a moment she looks up and listens, then returns to her thoughts and the Ring. Lightning flashes; the next thunder clap is closer to her mountain peak. Again she listens, and notices a dark cloud looming in her direction. As the cloud approaches, she sees a flying horse, bearing Valtrauta, one of her Valkyrie sisters. Brunnhilde jumps up overjoyed, and rushes to meet her, failing to notice Valtrauta's worried countenance. She begins to speak of her newly found pleasures and of Wotan, whom she assumes has forgiven her. But Valtrauta quickly tells her that she has not come to join in her foolish fate. On the contrary, she has come on an urgent secret mission, risking the wrath of Wotan. Terror of what is happening in Valhalla has forced her to plead for Brunnhilde's help in saving the gods.

Valtrauta recounts Wotan's wanderings, the shattering of his spear, and the felling of the World Ash, whose trunk and branches have been heaped around Valhalla. Wotan has now retreated into the hall of his castle where he sits in silence, surrounded by gods and heroes, his splintered spear in hand. Not even Freia's apples tempt him. "Fear and amazement make the gods seem frozen," Valtrauta says. His Valkyrie daughters sit at his feet, burdened by anguish and despair. Only the return of two ravens whom Wotan has set free will cause him to smile "a final time," if they bring back welcome news. Indeed, the gods are cursed by the Nibelung Ring; only Brunnhilde who now possesses the Ring can break the spell by giving it back to the Rhine Maidens. Valtrauta throws herself at Brunnhilde's feet and begs her to save her own kin.

Brunnhilde is shocked and explains that she can never part with the Ring with which Siegfried pledged his love. Far more than Valhalla's raptures, far more than any glory of the gods does she value this Ring. Its shining light reflects Siegfried's love. Never will she renounce love: "Rather let Valhalla crash to earth." She sends Valtrauta away despite her protests. As Valtrauta rushes off, the storm cloud rises from the nearby wood and vanishes in the distance amid thunder and lightning. Evening falls; from the valley the glimmering flames that guard Brunnhilde flicker in the dark.

Suddenly Brunnhilde notices that the flames are rising to an ever-higher pitch. "Siegfried!" she cries, and hastens joyfully to the edge of her rock to await his arrival. Siegfried leaps from the flames onto a high rock. Brunnhilde recoils and stares in astonishment at the figure to whom the magic helmet has given the appearance of Gunther. Siegfried, as Gunther, declares that he who is fearless of the fire has come to take Brunnhilde for his bride. The horrified Brunnhilde protests, thinking some demon has worked a spell to penetrate her stronghold. In despair she cries out Wotan's name, now believing her shame and sorrow to come from his curse.

Siegfried, still in the guise of Gunther, leaps from the rock and Brunnhilde extends her finger with the magic Ring, warning that it guards her safety. But Siegfried, undaunted, steps forward and forces the Ring from her finger. Brunnhilde frees herself from the struggle and flees, but Siegfried pursues her. Finally she drops to the ground. The Gunther-like Siegfried claims her as his bride and forces her into the cave. As she faints, Siegfried draws his sword and places it between them, so that he may keep his word to his blood brother that he would chastely woo Brunnhilde on Gunther's behalf.

ACT II

Near the river bank, before the great hall of the Gibichungs, sits Hagen. Spear in hand, and shield at his feet, he sleeps against a wall. It is night and the moon casts a faint light upon him. Close by rises a rocky cliff in which an altar has been carved to Fricka, Donner, and Wotan. Hagen's father, Alberich the dwarf, is crouching before him and whispering to him without awakening him. He reminds Hagen of his heritage from his mother as well as from him, and charges him to honor his father by seizing the Ring from Siegfried. Hagen, whom he brought up to live in hate, must now destroy Siegfried and ravish the Ring, thus avenging Alberich. In a dreamlike, almost hypnotic state, Hagen answers that he will do as Alberich commands. Slowly the dwarf withdraws and vanishes.

As the sun rises across the waters of the Rhine, Siegfried appears from the river bank, the magic helmet on his head. He approaches Hagen, who has now awakened. Gutrune joins them from the hall and Siegfried relates how he has won Brunnhilde for Gunther. Both will soon arrive by boat. After spending the night chastely beside Brunnhilde, he led her down the rocky mountain on the following morning. Gunther was waiting and quickly changed places with him without Brunnhilde's knowledge. The magic helmet, whose powers Hagen had taught him to use, changed Siegfried back to his true appearance and instantly returned him to the Gibichung kingdom. All agree that they should arrange a gracious welcome that will make Brunnhilde happy in her future home. Hagen rushes enthusiastically to call the men of the kingdom together and instruct them to prepare a great feast in honor of the coming wedding.

As the men begin merrily to make the preparations, the boat bearing Gunther and Brunnhilde appears in the distance. Some of the men rush to greet them and help them to land. Gunther leads Brunnhilde toward the hall, where Siegfried and Gutrune are standing. He greets them and expresses his gratitude for the good fortune that has brought the two couples together. Brunnhilde is astonished to see Siegfried. She starts toward him, then recoils in horror as she realizes that Siegfried is with Gutrune. She cries out to Siegfried, questioning why he is with this other woman; Siegfried simply answers that she is his bride, as Brunnhilde is Gunther's.

Brunnhilde, perceiving that Siegfried does not recognize her, grows faint. When Siegfried gestures with his hand, she sees the Ring on his finger. Trying to control her emotions, she asks him how this Ring has come to be on his hand, and asks Gunther where the Ring is that he forced her to give him. Siegfried answers that no woman gave him this Ring; he won it rightfully when he slew the dragon. Gunther, bewildered, answers that she gave him no Ring. Hagen steps into the quarrel; supporting Brunnhilde, he suggests that if she gave this Ring to her spouse, Siegfried must have obtained it through thievery.

The anguish of deceit and trickery tears through Brunnhilde's heart and she cries that she has been betrayed. Siegfried is her only spouse. But Siegfried denies

it, assuring Gunther that his sword Needful stood barrier
between him and Brunnhilde as he wooed her for his blood
brother. Brunnhilde vainly reminds Siegfried of the many
times earlier when his mighty sword hung on the wall
while its master was united with his true love. All present
demand that Siegfried tell them the truth. Has he shamed
the honor of Gunther? Siegfried tries to silence their
accusations. He places his hand on the head of Hagen's
spear and utters these fateful words:

> *Spear-point, hark to my words:*
> *If sharpness can pierce me,*
> *Yours be the point;*
> *And if death can overtake me,*
> *Yours be the blow —*
> *If I have wronged this bride,*
> *If I have betrayed my friend.*

Brunnhilde rushes forward to the spear herself and,
touching her hand to its head, swears an oath of her own:

> *Spear-point, hark to my words!*
> *I consecrate your strength*
> *To his undoing!*
> *And I dedicate your blade*
> *To his destruction!*
> *For he has broken all his vows*
> *And swears falsely even now.*

In an effort to understand this turn of events, Siegfried blames both himself, for the way he played the part
of Gunther, and the helmet, which he thinks may have only
partly disguised him. Brunnhilde's confusion will doubtless
vanish after she is wed. He urges the men to return to their
merrymaking and to proceed with the wedding preparations. Then, placing his arm around Gutrune, he retires to
the hall, leaving Brunnhilde, Gunther, and Hagen.

Brunnhilde begins to suspect a devil's plot, but
lacking an answer to the riddle, she asks for a sword with

which to sever her bonds with Siegfried. When Hagen
offers to avenge her, she laughs. How could he hope to conquer the mighty hero Siegfried? Besides, she has cast
spells on the noble warrior to protect him from all dangers
in battle except one. She confides to Hagen that she has
placed no protective spell on Siegfried's back, for he would
never show his back to a foe. Gunther, now doubting
Siegfried's conduct toward Brunnhilde, implores Hagen to
save his honor. Hagen takes up the challenge, noting that
his spear knows where to strike. Gunther reveals that his
only regret in Siegfried's death is the sorrow it will cause
his sister. His words shake Brunnhilde from her despair.
As if by some flash of insight, she realizes that Gutrune has
bewitched her lord and drawn him away.

Hagen and Gunther agree that Siegfried's death
should seem like an accident, so as to avoid Gutrune's reproaches. And so a hunting trip is planned for the morrow.
As they turn toward the great hall, they meet Siegfried,
Gutrune and the bridal procession. Gunther takes Brunnhilde's hand, and they follow in the procession, leaving
Hagen alone.

ACT III, Scene i

In the midst of the Rhine near a deserted, wooded
valley, the three Rhine Maidens swim to the surface and
sing of their lost Rhinegold. Siegfried's distant horn interrupts their reminiscences. They recognize him as he
approaches, and quickly take counsel before greeting him.
Siegfried has lost his way from the hunting party. He spies
the Maidens at the river's edge and rushes toward them,
asking whether they have seen an elfin creature who first
directed him toward game, then mischievously led him
astray. The Maidens ask what Siegfried is prepared to give
if they come to his aid. When he answers that he is booty-
less, they suggest the Ring on his finger. Siegfried laughs
and tells them that he slew a dragon to get the Ring; he is
hardly willing to exchange it for such meagre assistance
as he now needs. Besides, his wife would be angry if he

gave away his goods so frivolously.

In an effort to win his favor, the Rhine Maidens tease him coyly about his marriage and chide him for being henpecked. Siegfried joins the game; he holds the Ring out temptingly, then withdraws it. Soon the Maidens become solemn and grave. "Guard well," they warn, "for the Ring brings bad luck." Only the Rhine waves can wash away its curse. They tell Siegfried that Alberich stole the Ring's gold from the Rhine and that he forged the circlet to gain power for his selfish purposes. When it was taken from him, he cursed it. They warn that if Siegfried refuses to return the Ring, this day he will be slain.

Siegfried ignores their warnings, believing them to be like all women: cunning and eager to trick him out of his possession. He turns to leave, boasting that he is not afraid, for he has braved many battles and has always come out unscathed. The Ring may have granted him the lordship of the earth, but the grace of love wins it from him The Maidens could have had it, had they shown him love and affection rather than warning and foreboding.

He picks up a clod of earth and throws it behind him, declaring that he thinks no more highly of his life and limbs than he does of that earth. The Rhine Maidens hurriedly retreat, thinking him a fool. His sacred oaths he no longer keeps, yet the Ring, which will bring him death, he foolishly holds for his own. They swim away as Siegfried looks after them smiling.

Horns sound in the distance. Siegfried answers with his own, and presently Gunther, Hagen and the rest of the hunting party come to meet him. They pile their game in a heap, then settle down for refreshment. In response to Hagen's question, Siegfried admits that he has caught nothing during the hunt, though he nearly captured three "fair birds" who sang a warning that he would meet his death that day. Gunther, startled, fixes his eyes gloomily on Hagen. Hagen fills a horn with wine and passes it to Siegfried, inquiring mockingly about his reputation for understanding the language of birds. Siegfried drinks, then passes on the horn to Gunther and the other men before replying:

It's ages now
Since I heeded their chirps —
Since hearing the songs of women
My mind has forgotten the birds.

Feeling the effect of the wine, Siegfried offers to
sing tales of his youth. His song begins. He reviews his
life from the time Mime, the surly old dwarf, raised him
as an infant. He sings about the forging of the sword, the
slaying of the dragon, and the taking of the helmet and
Ring. As his tale approaches the present, Hagen interrupts and offers him another drink, laced with drops of
juice from an herb that will waken and brighten Siegfried's
memories. Continuing the story of his life, he recalls that
as soon as his tongue touched the dragon's blood he could
understand the songs of birds; and it was a bird that told
him of the sleeping goddess and led him to the fire-
encircled rock.

When he sings of his kiss, which awakened the
maiden, and of their loving embrace, Gunther springs forward in terror, flushing two ravens from a bush. They
circle above Siegfried, then fly toward the Rhine. Scornfully, Hagen asks whether Siegfried understands what
the ravens have said. Siegfried turns to look at the ravens
and stares blankly. His back is to Hagen, who shouts that
the birds have signaled vengeance. With these words he
aims his spear at Siegfried's back. Gunther tries to catch
Hagen's arm but he is too late. Siegfried swings around in
an effort to defend himself, but his strength fails and he
falls on his shield. Hagen turns coolly away and walks off,
while the anguished Gunther bends over Siegfried and
hears his dying words.

Brunnhilde . . .
The joyful Brunnhilde smiles!
Her radiant eye forever open!
Her sweet breath, gently wafting!
Blissful is my departure . . .
Brunnhilde welcomes me now.

He sinks back and dies. Gunther gestures to his men to bear Siegfried's body away. As night falls, the solemn procession recedes into the mist that rises from the Rhine.

Scene ii

Back in the Gibichung's great hall, Gutrune comes out of her chamber, attracted by the sound of a distant horn. Wild dreams have troubled her; she cannot sleep. The horn sounds again, and soon Hagen's voice is heard, shouting for all to awaken and receive the returning hunters. As the men and women assemble with torches, the train bearing Siegfried's body approaches. Hagen tells Gutrune that Siegfried will never again hunt, fight, nor look for ladies' love — a savage boar has slain him. She shrieks and falls on the body as Gunther steps forward to comfort her. Horrified, she cries that her brother and his men have murdered Siegfried. Gunther answers that Hagen was the boar who gored the hero.

Hagen, questioning why they should be angry with him for having settled their debt, admits that he was the slayer, and demands the magic Ring as the prize for his deed. Gunther protests, claiming that it is Gutrune's dowry. Hagen draws his sword and rushes at him. Despite the onlookers, who try to stop the ensuing struggle, Hagen strikes Gunther a mortal blow. As Gutrune screams, Hagen tries to seize the Ring from Siegfried's hand. But the hand rises threateningly, and all remain spellbound with horror. At this moment Brunnhilde enters.

Stern and calm, Brunnhilde chastises all of them for quarrelling when they should be honoring the noblest man that ever lived. Silencing Gutrune's cries of woe, Brunnhilde tells her that she was never Siegfried's wife, only his mistress. Brunnhilde is his wife; to her Siegfried pledged his eternal devotion long before he had seen Gutrune. In desperation, Gutrune turns on Hagen, accusing him of urging her to make the treacherous drink that drew Siegfried to her. "I see it all now! Brunnhilde was his true love; the cup compelled him to forget!" Turning away in shame, she moves from Siegfried's body and bends over the body of her fallen brother.

Brunnhilde orders the men to build a mighty funeral pyre on the bank of the Rhine, and to bring her faithful horse, Grane. As the young men hurriedly build the pyre, the women deck it with herbs and flowers. Brunnhilde remains rapt in contemplation of Siegfried's body.

"Like the brilliant sun does he radiate toward me; the purest was he, yet he betrayed me." So Brunnhilde begins her beautiful eulogy to Siegfried. He was loyal in his bond of friendship, yet he failed in his pledge of love to Brunnhilde. As she continues to gaze transfixed at him, she perceives the full import of their destiny. No one was truer than Siegfried, yet he was the victim of his self-made fate. He was a free instrument in Wotan's master plan, but because of his failure, both he and Wotan must perish. Through the pain and shock of Siegfried's death, Brunnhilde becomes aware that the time has now come for the gods to end their reign.

She signals to the men to place Siegfried's body on the funeral pyre, then takes the Ring from his finger and contemplates it. The fatal Ring has come back to Brunnhilde, but now she understands the curse of which the Rhine Maidens spoke. To them in the nearby river she calls, "What you desire, you soon shall have." From her ashes, the Rhine's waters will reclaim the Ring and cleanse it of its curse forever.

She places the Ring on her finger, then takes a huge firebrand from one of the men. With a cry to the ravens to fly home to their ruler and tell him what they have heard and witnessed by the Rhine, she flings the torch into the pyre. She commands the ravens to travel by way of her mountain abode and bid Loge, who still masters the fiery circle, to hasten to Valhalla. The gods' twilight has come at last. The funeral pyre bursts into wild flames. The two ravens disappear in the heavens. Grane is led forward, and Brunnhilde rushes to embrace him. She whispers to

him of the rapture they will soon know as they sacrifice
themselves to be with their hero. She unbridles the horse,
then springs onto his back with the cry:

> *Heiajaho! Grane!*
> *Give greeting to your master*
> *Siegfried! Siegfried! See!*
> *Joyfully your wife greets you.*

They leap into the burning pyre; the flames burst
forth with such intensity that the whole hall begins to
burn. Terrified, the men and women back away. As the
glow subsides, a cloud of smoke ascends from the remains
and the Rhine overflows its banks in a mighty flood. In the
waves swim the Rhine Maidens who appear on the spot
where the fire has been extinguished. Hagen, hovering
anxiously nearby, is suddenly seized with alarm. He
realizes that the Rhine Maidens are about to reclaim the
Ring. He throws aside his spear, shield and helmet and
rushes like a madman into the flooding river. Two of the
Maidens seize him by the neck and draw him down into the
watery depths. The third, swimming off in front of the
others, holds the Ring aloft.

Through the bank of smoking clouds on the horizon,
a red glow of light becomes visible. Its brightness increases
and illuminates the Rhine Maidens, who swim off into the
distance, merrily rejoicing with their Ring. The waters of
the Rhine subside and return to the river's bed. From the
scorched ruins of the Gibichung's hall, the men and women
look with growing agitation and alarm toward the light in
the heavens. Gradually they see Valhalla, in which the gods
and heroes are sitting as if they were statues, while flames
mount around them and consume the mighty edifice with
all its glory. Dispelling the anguish and turmoil, swelling
strains of music herald an act of redemption through love.

Parsifal

ACT I

Deep in the sacred forest that surrounds the castle of the Grail, an elderly knight and two squires lie sleeping under a tree. As day breaks, the solemn morning reveille sounds from the distant castle. The elderly knight, Gurnemanz, is the first to rise. Vigorously he shakes the young sleepers, who spring up, ashamed that he is up and about before them. As is the custom, Gurnemanz leads them in morning prayer. Then he instructs them to make ready for the arrival of their leader, who will soon be brought to the nearby lake for his bath.

Seeing two knights approach from the castle, Gurnemanz asks how Amfortas fares. He wonders if the herb Gawaine acquired with such hardship has brought relief to the suffering king? The knights report that Amfortas' pain has returned in full strength after a brief respite; he has passed a sleepless night, and now seeks what comfort the waters of this holy sanctuary can give. Gurnemanz shakes his head sorrowfully, and reminds the knights that their efforts are bound to fail, for though knights have searched far and wide for a healing medicament, only one thing and one man can help.

As Gurnemanz turns away, a young squire spies a frenzied woman on horseback riding into their midst. The knights recognize Kundry as she flings herself from her horse and rushes up to Gurnemanz. She is wildly clad; her black hair is dishevelled, and the intensity of her dark piercing eyes reveal the urgency of her errand. Quickly she hands Gurnemanz a small crystal flask, and explains that it contains balsam from Arabia. Then, exhausted from her travels, she collapses and falls to the ground.

A train of squires and knights approaches, bearing a litter on which Amfortas lies. His once-stately figure is twisted and ravaged by pain, but he manages to raise himself a little to ask for Gawaine. When he learns that Gawaine has gone off in search of another herb, he despairs, knowing that Klingsor's ensnarements are everywhere. He pleads with the knights not to risk such dangers for his sake. There is nothing to be done but to wait for the promised one, the one who is enlightened by "pity" — "the naive and pure one." Gurnemanz approaches Amfortas and hands him Kundry's flask. Amfortas agrees to try the balsam and thanks Kundry for her service.

The procession moves on to the lake in the valley, leaving Gurnemanz, Kundry, and a few squires in the forest clearing. The young men are suspicious of the savage-like woman, but Gurnemanz reproaches them. What harm has she done them, she who seeks only to serve the knights of the Grail? Who is it that carries tidings to distant lands where comrades are fighting; who runs errands and brings help in times of danger and need; who but Kundry? Yet she has never asked for their thanks. In times past she was under a pagan curse, he explains, but now she makes this sacred realm her home, seeking to atone for her former sins. Thus Kundry serves her own soul while she serves the brotherhood. It was Titurel, the former king of the Grail who first found her lying in this wood, stiff and rigid as in death. But when she was awakened, her ageless body was miraculously revived and she was ready to serve. Long has she been in their midst; it is not her presence but her absence that should be feared. For each time she has remained away, misfortune has fallen upon them. Indeed, on that sorrowful day when Amfortas lost the holy Spear, Kundry had been off on one of her travels. Only afterwards did Gurnemanz find her, as Titurel had, exhausted and frozen in her death-like sleep.

The squires question Gurnemanz about the Spear, and he recalls for them the fateful day when Amfortas carried the hallowed relic into battle against Klingsor. Near the sorcerer's stronghold, a maid of exquisite beauty

tempted and seduced their king. As he laid aside the Spear
in order to embrace her, Klingsor appeared without warning, grasped the sacred weapon and thrust it into Amfortas'
side, so inflicting the fateful wound that does not heal.
Though Gurnemanz had rushed to the young king's aid,
the laughing Klingsor fled with the Spear before they could
stop him. Pressed by the squires to reveal more, Gurnemanz
relates the story of the Grail and the Spear.

> *The sacred vessel, the holy cup*
> *From which He drank at the Last Supper,*
> *In which His blood divine was caught —*
> *This and the Spear that shed His blood,*
> *God's messenger placed in Titurel's hold.*
> *He built a shrine in which to keep*
> *These relics, both of worth untold.*
> *You who are chosen for their service*
> *Must take the path no sinner treads,*
> *For well you know: into the brotherhood*
> *Only the pure can be admitted.*
> *Then blessed by the Grail's forces and powers,*
> *The knighthood works for all mankind.*

Klingsor could not win admittance to the brotherhood of the Grail, however long and hard he tried. Unable
to overcome the sin of lust, he emasculated himself in an
effort to achieve purity and gain entrance to the sacred
knighthood. But by this very act, he removed the possibility of overcoming his desires, and thus the Grail's guardian was forced to drive him away. Thereafter Klingsor
learned how his ignominious deed could be used to serve
evil through sorcery and black magic. In what was formerly a desert not far from the Grail kingdom, he created a
luxuriant, bewitching garden; in its midst he placed beautiful women endowed with infernal charms. There they
wait to entice the Grail's true knights to their ruin, for
once fully in Klingsor's power, the knights are forced to
remain his vassals forever.

When the pious Titurel reached old age, he passed

the guardianship of the Grail and Spear to his son, Amfortas, who impetuously presumed to conquer the evil Klingsor. Thus it was that Amfortas fell into the evil master's trap. The captured Spear gives Klingsor power over even the most holy. The Grail itself, he reckons, will soon be his; then his power will be limitless.

The young squires vow to regain the Spear, but Gurnemanz repeats that only one man can do so. After Amfortas lost the Spear, he knelt in the castle sanctuary, praying for protection and a sign of what must be done. A heavenly voice answered him:

> *The pure and foolish one,*
> *Made wise through compassion —*
> *Wait for him*
> *Whom I have chosen.*

The squires, in deep contemplation, repeat the prophetic words.

Cries of knights rushing from the woods interrupt the story. A wild swan flutters feebly overhead, then drops to the ground dying. The squires and knights lift the fallen swan, horrified that anyone could have shot it in this hallowed forest. An unknown boy is found and brought forward. When asked whether he is the hunter whose arrow pierced the bird, he answers at once that he is, and boasts that he can hit anything that flies.

Gurnemanz scolds the youth and asks if he has not found all the beasts and birds in this place friendly and tame. Had the swan harmed him? The boy realizes that his act was senseless and cruel; he bows his head in shame and admits that he did not know his deed was wrong. Upon further questioning, he confesses that he does not know how he came to this part of the woods. He does not know who his father is, nor can he tell them his own name. He knows only that he has a mother who reared him all alone in the woods and on the barren moors. Her name is Herzeleide — Heart's Sorrow. And as for his simple bow and arrows, he himself made them for protection on his wanderings through the forest.

Gurnemanz recognizes by the boy's bearing that he is of noble birth, and wonders why his mother could not find a better weapon for him. Still lying on the ground nearby, Kundry has watched the boy with deep interest. She breaks her silence to call out that his mother bore him after his father, the valiant knight Gamuret, was slain in battle. In order to protect her son from a similar death, she reared him without knowledge of weapons or of worldly matters. Thus the foolish mother reared a foolish boy.

Once when the boy was on the outskirts of the woods, Kundry continues, he saw a glittering array of knights on horseback. Attracted by their splendor and longing for adventure, he tried to pursue them; but unable to overtake them, he lost his way and wandered aimlessly for many days and nights. During his wanderings, robbers and giants encountered his strength, and the wicked learned to fear him.

Gurnemanz asks if his mother does not yearn and grieve for him. It is Kundry who answers. "Herzeleide grieves no more. She is dead. As I rode through the woods I witnessed her death."

On hearing this, the enraged boy seizes Kundry by the throat and begins to shake her. Gurnemanz pulls him away and reproves him for his violence. The dazed youth stands motionless while Gurnemanz tells him that Kundry never lies; what she relates is what she knows. Trembling with grief and shock, the boy sinks to the ground. Kundry rushes to a spring in the woods and returns with water, which she sprinkles on his forehead, then hands him the container from which to drink. Gurnemanz commends her, for just so does the Grail teach mercy. "He triumphs who meets evil with good." But Kundry turns away sadly. "Good do I never. I seek only to rest, for I am weary." She moves to a deserted spot behind a thicket and lies down.

The procession bearing Amfortas returns from the lake. Gurnemanz turns to the boy and, looking deeply into his eyes, bids him join the holy festival that is about to take place. He gently places his arm around his shoulder and leads him away. He tells him that because he is pure, the communion of the Grail will sustain him and give him strength. "Who is the Grail?" asks Parsifal, but Gurnemanz answers that he is forbidden to say. Only he who is foreordained can find his way into its presence, yet knowledge of the sacred vessel will not be withheld from one who is called to serve it. Indeed, no earthly road to the Grail kingdom is known. Thus no man can find it who is not guided to it.

While Gurnemanz and Parsifal walk, the forest around them gradually changes. They pass through a gateway into the side of a rocky precipice, and are lost from sight. Soon they reappear, ascending through stony passages until at last they reach a large hall. High overhead floats a glittering dome, supported by mighty pillars which also mark the entrances to many corridors. From the heights can be heard the sound of chimes. The boy stands spellbound; Gurnemanz charges him to observe and learn from the sight he is about to behold.

The Grail knights enter in solemn procession, and move to their places at the long tables that form a circle within the hall. They sing of the communion in which they will partake.

For holy communion
We prepare each day,
As though for the last time
It might bless us.
He who lives to do good deeds
May approach this meal
Time and again,
And receive its sustenance —
The purest gift.

From one of the corridors Amfortas is carried in on his litter. Before him march squires who bear a shrine draped in a red-violet covering. The procession moves to the center of the circle, where an altar stands. The squires place the shrine on the altar and those who bear the litter help Amfortas onto a raised couch behind the altar. Silence falls as the knights take their seats. From a distant arched niche behind Amfortas' throne the voice of Titurel can be heard. He urges Amfortas to perform his duty and uncover the shrine. Amfortas resists. He begs his father to assume once again the high office of guardian of the Grail, for he, Amfortas, is no longer worthy of its service. The pain the Grail's presence causes him is more than he can bear. Again Titurel commands him to fulfill his duty, assuring him that in the service of the Grail he will overcome the guilt he has incurred.

Amfortas raises himself obediently and unveils the Grail; then trembling, he bows in silent prayer before the sacred vessel. A blinding ray of light descends upon it, and the crystal cup begins to glow with ever-increasing luster. Angel voices sing from above:

> *Take this my blood*
> *For the sake of our love.*
> *Take this my body*
> *In remembrance of me.*

Amfortas raises the Grail aloft and moves it slowly toward one side of the hall, then toward the other, consecrating the bread and wine on the tables before which the knights now kneel. As he sets the sacred vessel down, its glow gradually fades; the squires cover it and return it to the shrine. The knights seat themselves and prepare to eat the bread and drink the wine. Gurnemanz, who has kept a vacant place beside him, signals to the newcomer to take part in the communion. But the boy remains standing, silent and motionless as if in a trance. Nor does Amfortas partake of the communion. He has sunk exhausted upon his cushions. Bowing his head, he places his hand on his wound, which has begun to bleed again, and cries out in agony. The youth clutches his heart, as if experiencing Amfortas' suffering as his own.

After the communion, the knights prepare for the recessional, and move slowly from the hall. Amfortas' litter is borne away; only Gurnemanz and the young stranger remain. The elder knight, disappointed by the boy's failure to respond to the ceremony, shakes him by the arm. Calling him "nothing but a fool," he directs him from the hall and shuts the door angrily behind him. Then he too turns and leaves, following after the other knights.

ACT II

In a tower of his castle sits the evil Klingsor, gazing into a metal mirror. He is surrounded by the instruments of his magic. The time has come to lure the simple, wandering boy into his snare. He concentrates on his necromantic implements, making mysterious gestures over them and over the depths below. He cries out to Kundry, who, still subject to his curse, is unable to defy his bidding.

> *Rise up! Come to me!*
> *Your master calls, nameless one!*
> *She-devil! Rose of Hell!*
> *Gundryggia then, Kundry now:*
> *Approach me, Kundry!*
> *Your master bids you here!*

From out of a bluish vapor, the somnambulant form of Kundry appears. She utters an anguished cry, as if half-awakened from a nightmare. Klingsor chides her for mingling with the knights of the Grail. Do they not treat her as no more than a poor beast? What does she seek from them? They are weak before the mighty Klingsor and his seductive Kundry. And now the two of them will encounter their most challenging foe. For it is indeed an elusive enemy whose shield is innocence.

Despite Kundry's protests, Klingsor insists that she will and must do as he commands. His power over her is unique because he alone is immune to her temptations. With a laugh, she mocks Klingsor's chastity. The pain of untamed desire, which he brutally repressed, taunts him anew through her devilish jeers. He silences her, warning that he has vanquished the holiest of knights and soon will make himself master of the all-powerful Grail. Lamenting her fate, Kundry demands to know when she will be released from Klingsor's curse. He answers that only he who rejects her can set her free and sarcastically suggests that it may be her next victim.

Klingsor spies the handsome youth approaching the castle. He sounds a horn, calling his watchmen and soldiers to guard their beautiful young playmates. As the unsuspecting wanderer enters the grounds, Klingsor's knights challenge him, but he easily wounds one after the other and finally forces them to flee. Kundry vanishes amid Klingsor's laughter, while he and his tower disappear behind a vaporous screen.

The youth, now alone, looks about in astonishment; he finds himself in a lush tropical garden surrounded by castle walls. From all sides beautiful maidens rush in, their garments thrown hastily about them as if they had been startled from sleep. They cry out, accusing him of wounding their beloved companions. Delighted by their charms, he greets them and naively marvels at their beauty. The maidens bemoan the loss of their injured playmates, but he seeks to console them and offers to join their games. The mourning of the maids turns to seductive merriment. One by one they slip away to adorn themselves with flowers from the garden. Soon a quarrel breaks out among them, each demanding the attractive stranger for herself, and eagerly offering herself to him. Bewildered by their attention and annoyed by their bickering, he tries to escape.

Suddenly a voice calls out. "Parsifal!" He breaks away in surprise and stands motionless as the name is repeated. It is the name his mother once called him. Slowly Kundry comes toward him. Once again, as the unwilling vassal of Klingsor, she appears as an exquisitely beautiful woman. The flower-decked maidens are startled. At Kundry's stern command they withdraw reluctantly from the garden. Overcome by her loveliness, the bemused youth asks why she names him thus, he who has no name.

She explains that she has called him Parsifal, the "foolish pure one," for so did his father name him when he lay dying on a battlefield in Arabia. It is to reveal this that she has waited here so long for his coming. She had seen him when he was a mere infant at his mother's breast and witnessed the care and love lavished upon him. She knew of his mother's suffering at the time of his father's death, and of her fear that Parsifal, too, might one day die before his time in mortal combat. When as a grown boy he left his forest home, his mother waited for endless days and nights. Tormented by fear and anguish over what might have befallen him, she died at last of a broken heart.

Parsifal, reminded again of his thoughtless action toward his mother, sinks down at Kundry's feet and weeps. As though soothing a child, she touches his forehead. Then with gentle compassion she embraces him and offers him her love. Assuring him that his mother sends her blessing from heaven in this first kiss of love, she bends to touch her lips to his. But Parsifal, suddenly awakened as if from a spell, tears himself from her. Struck by a fearful realization, he presses his hand to his heart.

> *Amfortas!*
> *The wound! The wound!*
> *It burns in my heart!*
> *Oh misery! Misery!*
> *From the innermost depths of my soul*
> *It cries aloud!*

The vivid memory of the suffering Amfortas with his bleeding wound arises before him. He recalls the vision of the holy Grail with its sublime glow of redemption. This picture stills the passion that Kundry has awakened in him. He sinks to his knees in deep meditation. Now at last he understands the revelation of that pure, radiant light that streamed from the Grail. In this was contained Christ's plea that His sacred cup be delivered from sinful, unclean hands. Parsifal cries aloud:

The divine lamentation
Sounded through my soul
Fearfully loud and clear,
While I, the foolish coward, fled
To wild and childish deeds.

Kundry, whose astonishment has changed to sorrowful wonder, approaches the kneeling Parsifal. Cautiously she leans over to caress him and urge him to find solace in her loving embrace. He gazes blankly at her and realizes that in just such a way Amfortas had succumbed to her overpowering temptation. Quickly he rises and pushes her away. She bemoans his cruelty and begs his help, telling him that she is tormented by a curse which haunts her day and night and will follow her even into death. Once she beheld the Christ and laughed at Him; but when His glance met hers she was filled with an eternal longing. Since then she has sought Him from life to life and world to world. Knowing now that Parsifal has experienced Him, she pleads for salvation. If he will but join his being with hers for one hour, she too may be cleansed and delivered. Parsifal refuses, aware that such a search for sacred bliss would bring both their souls into damnation. But he offers her redemption if she will show him the way back to Amfortas.

Kundry flies into a rage and laughs at his madness. Again she pleads for one single hour with him. He thrusts her aside as she tries once more to embrace him. Shrieking with frenzy, she curses all paths and roads along which he might seek to find his way back to the kingdom of the Grail.

Suddenly Klingsor appears on a rampart of the castle, brandishing the sacred Spear. With careful aim, he hurls it at Parsifal. The Spear flies toward the youth, then halts miraculously above his head. Parsifal seizes it and with ecstasy and triumph holds it aloft. Gripping the shaft firmly he makes the sign of the cross and proclaims the end of Klingsor's magic powers. As though shaken by an earthquake, the castle falls into ruin. The gardens wither and only a desert remains. The maidens, who had rushed out

in alarm, lie scattered about like shrivelled flowers. Kundry
cries out and falls to the ground. As Parsifal starts to leave,
he turns and calls to her: "Thou knowest where thou canst
find me again!" Then he hastens away.

ACT III

Gurnemanz, now much older, is living as a hermit
in a meadow near the Grail castle. His abode is a crude
wooden hut built against the side of a rock. Still wearing
the tunic of a Grail knight over his faded hermit robe, he
emerges from his hut into the quiet sunlit morning. All at
once he is aware of groaning sounds that seem to come
from a thicket where the meadow meets the forest. The animal-like cries are somehow familiar. He approaches the
brambles and parts them in order to see what creature
lies there.

He recognizes Kundry, who continues to moan and
toss as if awakening from a bad dream. Except for the
occasional movement, she remains in her rigid death-like
sleep. Gurnemanz sets about to revive her. At last she
opens her eyes and stares intently at him. She is dishevelled
and wildly dressed as before, but the wildness has faded
from her expression. She rises, smoothes her hair and
straightens her dress. Immediately she asks if she may
help him. "Service . . . service," she begs. Sadly, Gurnemanz lets her know that her service will be light; for no
longer do the knights need her to run errands or seek herbs
for their king. Much has changed; now, everyone fends
for himself.

As Kundry moves about, Gurnemanz marvels at the
change in her. Her manner is serene, and he senses an
earnest humility that was never there before. Perhaps it
is the miraculous effect of this holy day, for it is Good
Friday morning.

Kundry fetches a pitcher from the hut and goes into
the meadow to fill it at the nearby spring. Glancing into
the woods, she sees a knight approaching and points him
out to Gurnemanz. The knight's armor is black; the visor

of his helmet is closed, and he carries a lowered spear at
his side. With bowed head he moves slowly toward them,
then stops to sit down on a grassy mound near the spring.
As though caught in a dream, he looks about him uncer-
tainly. After observing him at some length, Gurnemanz
steps forward to greet him. Parsifal acknowledges the
greeting merely by slowly shaking his head. The old hermit
informs him that he is on sacred ground, where it is forbidden to bear arms, and most particularly on this holy
day. Parsifal only bows his head. Gurnemanz urges him
sternly to disarm, whereupon Parsifal rises and thrusts
the Spear into the ground. He puts aside his shield and
sword, removes his helmet, and kneels before the Spear
in silent prayer. Gurnemanz stares at him with wonder
and is seized by sudden emotion. He beckons to Kundry.
Does she not recognize him? It is the lad who once killed
the swan, the foolish one whom he, himself, once dismissed in anger. In awe Gurnemanz gazes long at the
Spear, aware at last of what it is that stands before him.

Parsifal rises from his prayer and looks calmly at the
old knight. Recognizing Gurnemanz, he extends his hand
in greeting and thanks God that he has at last found his
way to him. He tells him that he seeks Amfortas, from
whom as an innocent fool he turned away, but for whose
healing he knows himself ordained. He relates the tale
of his wanderings. Always his paths were cursed and
he was ever near despair, not knowing whether he could
protect the holy Spear and return it to the Grail's kingdom. Time and again he won in battle, but never bearing
the Spear, which has remained undefiled. Overwhelmed
by joy and gratitude, Gurnemanz praises the good fortune
that has brought Parsifal back at last. Amfortas, more
tortured and tormented than ever, has for some time re-
fused to fulfill his office and to unveil the holy vessel.
Since he cannot die so long as he beholds the Grail's light,
he will not unveil it, so that he may hasten his end. The
brotherhood, deprived of the holy meal, has withered in
strength and courage. Many have departed. The old king,
Titurel, no longer quickened by the light of the Grail, is
dead.

Deeply grieved, Parsifal blames himself for the suffering caused by his own blindness and foolishness. He
sinks dejected onto the grassy knoll. Kundry brings a basin
of water and begins to moisten his brow. Gurnemanz stops
her and bids her use the water from the blessed spring
to purify him and wash away the stains of his travels.
They help Parsifal to the edge of the spring and remove
his outer garments. As Kundry bathes his feet, Parsifal
asks if he can be guided to Amfortas. Gurnemanz assures
him that he will be. Indeed, this very day, Amfortas must
once again perform his long-neglected office, to sanctify
his father's body before its burial. Gurnemanz sprinkles
the holy water from the spring onto Parsifal's head as if
in blessing, while Kundry takes a golden flask from her
bosom, pours some of its contents upon his feet, then
dries them with her hair. Parsifal gently removes the vial
from Kundry's hand. Passing it to Gurnemanz, he asks to
be anointed king of the Grail. Gurnemanz empties the
flask over Parsifal's head, then folds his hands above his
head in blessing. Thus it was foretold, he recalls, that
Gurnemanz would bless the king. Parsifal, in turn, scoops
water from the spring and baptizes the kneeling Kundry
in the name of the Redeemer. Kundry bows her head and
weeps.

The fields and meadows glow with an unprecedented
light and beauty. The air's sweetness and tenderness
recall childhood days and joys to Parsifal. It is the Good
Friday spell, explains Gurnemanz. The spirits of nature
have not the power to experience the Redeemer on the
cross; so they smile upon redeemed man who has been
cleansed by divine love and sacrifice. As God pitied and
spared man, so man in turn learns to spare nature and
treads with care upon the meadow flowers and grass.
Grateful to man for his enlightened role as her protector,
nature wakes to her day of innocence. Moistened by the
joyful tears of redeemed man, she glows with rare fresh-
ness and beauty. Thus Kundry's tears fall like blessed dew
and cause the landscape to shine more sweetly.

As distant bells sound the midday hour, Gurnemanz

tells them that it is time to leave. He brings from his hut
a mantle of the knights of the Grail, which he and Kundry
place on the young knight. Parsifal solemnly grasps the
Spear, and with Kundry follows Gurnemanz into the forest.
The pealing of the bells grows ever louder as they walk
along paths and rocky passages toward the stately hall of
the Grail castle. As they pass through its doors, they see
the mourning knights bearing Titurel's coffin; from a second entrance, other knights carry Amfortas on his litter,
preceded by the covered shrine of the Grail. The funeral
bier is placed beneath the center of the dome, and Amfortas is carried to the throne as before. One after the
other the knights enter the hall. The coffin is opened;
Amfortas raises himself high on his couch and stares at
the body of his father. He implores Titurel's spirit to inter-
cede before the Saviour so that he, Amfortas, may be released from life. The knights urge him to unveil the holy
cup; but at the last moment, Amfortas draws back and begs
the knights to run him through with their swords, sparing
him this insufferable task. They recoil in horror.

Fearful and trembling, Amfortas struggles to his feet.
At this moment, Parsifal, Gurnemanz and Kundry enter the
hall unnoticed. The holy Spear outstretched, Parsifal approaches Amfortas and with its sacred point touches the
wound in his side. "Only one weapon serves; the Spear that
smote must heal," he says. Amfortas' face shines with
rapture. He staggers, overcome with bliss and awe, as
Gurnemanz supports him. The knights gaze intently at
Parsifal, who moves to the center of the hall and holds
the Spear aloft.

> *Be healed, cleansed and forgiven of sin!*
> *For now I administer your high office.*
>> *Blessed be your pain and suffering,*
>> *Which awoke the force of compassion*
>> *And changed my foolhardy thoughts*
>> *Into purest, powerful wisdom.*
>> *The holy Spear —*
>> *Once more behold in this.*

Parsifal turns to the shrine of the Grail and instructs the squires to open it. Slowly he takes the cup and kneels in silent prayer. The Grail glows with a brilliant light and its golden aura shines over all. Momentarily brought to life, Titurel rises from his coffin and lifts his hand in benediction, then sinks back. From the dome above, a white dove descends and hovers over Parsifal's head. Spellbound by this vision, Kundry gazes at Parsifal and, her torment at an end, falls dead. Amfortas and Gurnemanz kneel in homage before Parsifal, who lifts the Grail in blessing before the assembled brotherhood. The knights join them in their thankful prayer: "Miracle of highest grace: Redemption for the Redeemer."

Notes

1. "A Communication to My Friends," *Richard Wagner's Prose Works*, translated by William Ashton Ellis (New York, Broude Brothers, 1966), Volume I, pp. 357-358.

2. *Ibid.*, p. 357.

3. *Ibid.*, p. 361.

4. *Ibid.*, p. 366.

5. Briefwechsel Zwischen Wagner und Liszt (Druck und Verlag von Breitkopf und Härtel, 1900), p. 155.

6. "Art and Revolution," *Richard Wagner's Prose Works*, Volume I, p. 47.

7. "Music of the Future," *Richard Wagner's Prose Works*, Volume III, pp. 306-307.

8. "Art and Revolution," *op. cit.*, p. 34.

9. König Ludwig II und Richard Wagner Briefwechsel (Karlsruhe i.B., G. Braun, Verlag, 1939), Volume III, p. 159.

10. *Ibid.*, p. 182.

11. Arthur M. Abell, *Talks With Great Composers* (New York, Philosophical Library, 1955), p. 58.

12. *The Writings of Ralph Waldo Emerson* (New York, Modern Library, Random House, 1940), p. 40.

13. Carl Gustav Jung, *Psychology and Alchemy* (New York, Pantheon Books, 1953), p. 170.